An Introduction to

CLASSICAL AND CONTEMPORARY SOCIAL THEORY:

A Critical Perspective

THE REYNOLDS SERIES IN SOCIOLOGY

Larry T. Reynolds, *Editor*

by **GENERAL HALL, INC.**

An Introduction to

CLASSICAL AND CONTEMPORARY SOCIAL THEORY:

A Critical Perspective

Berch Berberoglu
University of Nevada, Reno

GENERAL HALL, INC.
Publishers
5 Talon Way
Dix Hills, New York 11746

29865354

An Introduction to
CLASSICAL AND CONTEMPORARY SOCIAL THEORY:
A Critical Perspective

GENERAL HALL, INC.
5 Talon Way
Dix Hills, New York 11746

Publisher: Ravi Mehra
Composition: Graphics Division, General Hall, Inc.

LIBRARY OF CONGRESS CATALOG CARD NUMBER: **92–76215**

ISBN: 1–882289–06–4 [paper]
1–882289–07–2 [cloth]

Manufactured in the United States of America

Contents

PREFACE AND ACKNOWLEDGMENTS

Social theory is an essential tool that scholars use in their analysis of society. Just as without thinking we cannot make sense of the world around us, without the use of theory facts in their raw form remain unintelligible and disjointed to all but the purest of the pure empiricists, who reject the use of theory altogether. The adoption of a theoretical approach in social analysis, especially one that is critical and challenges long-held assumptions about the social world, is therefore an important first step in developing an informed understanding of society through social research.

My interest in social theory goes back more than two decades, when I was first introduced to the great social theorists of the nineteenth and early twentieth centuries in my undergraduate theory course taught by Larry Reynolds at Central Michigan University in the early 1970s. It is through his inspiring and engaging lectures on Emile Durkheim, Max Weber, Karl Marx, and other giants of classical social theory that I came to confront some of the central social issues of our time. Later, in a graduate seminar on contemporary social theory, I learned from Larry about the raging controversies in American sociology—from its early beginnings to the Chicago School to Talcott Parsons, Robert Merton, and other proponents of modern functionalism, which dominated the postwar academic scene, to C. Wright Mills and the critical and radical theorizing and activism of a new generation of sociologists in the 1960s who made an important and lasting contribution to the discipline.

The knowledge I gained through my formal theoretical training in these formative years, however, goes much beyond what I learned about individual theorists, for my broad exposure to social theory during this critical period helped establish a solid foundation for my theoretical studies in the years that followed. For his pivotal role in introducing me to some of the central theoretical positions that I have come to adopt over the years, and in this way for setting me on a most valuable intellectual journey, I thank my mentor, colleague,

vii

and friend Larry Reynolds in appreciation of his contribution to my theoretical development.

During my graduate studies in the early to mid-1970s, first at the State University of New York at Binghamton and then at Central Michigan University, where I attended seminars and courses taught by James Petras and Blain Stevenson, respectively, and later at the University of Oregon, where I studied toward my doctoral degree under Albert Szymanski, my exposure to and interest in social theory, centered in political economy and class analysis, came to define the parameters of my theoretical orientation in sociology. In this more mature period in my thinking I came to adopt a more developed, dialectical conception of social analysis informed by the principles of historical materialism. It was also during this most critical period in my intellectual development that I began to see the central, indeed most fundamental, role played by social class in society. Analysis of class structure, class conflict, and class struggle, defined in terms of relations of production, became the basis of my approach to social theory and social research that continues to inform my theoretical perspective and intellectual work. Throughout this book, the analysis of the positions of each of the classical and contemporary theorists discussed is carried out from the vantage point of this most fundamental social phenomenon—*class*.

This book was written with the aim of introducing to the beginning college student some of the major classical and contemporary social theorists of the late nineteenth and early twentieth centuries. Given both the number of prominent social theorists and the scope of the issues addressed over the past century, this book is necessarily selective in both focus and depth of analysis of questions raised by a select number of theorists I have decided to cover. Moreover, the analysis presented is both interpretative and critical in its approach toward the subject matter. It is hoped that such an approach will stimulate interest in the beginning student to ponder the critical issues raised by these theorists in a fresh new way. In this sense, the book is not intended as a definitive text in social theory but as a supplemental guide for use in introductory sociology and social theory courses to help familiarize students with the works of some of the most prominent social theorists of our time.

The sixteen chapters that make up this book were designed to be brief, concise, and to the point, expressed whenever possible in the words of the theorists concerned so that the central ideas of each of these theorists can be presented in their original form. Thus this introductory book on social theory was designed to serve as an initial stepping-stone to more in-depth analyses of these and other theorists usually covered in more advanced texts specifically prepared for advanced undergraduate theory courses in sociology. If this book succeeds in stimulating in the beginning student a modicum of interest in social theory—one that will lead to further theoretical studies—then the purpose for which this project was originally conceived and undertaken will be worth all the effort I have put into it.

Over the years, many colleagues have contributed to the formation and development of the ideas presented in these pages and thus have contributed, directly or indirectly, to the success of this undertaking. I would like to thank Jim Salt, Walda Katz-Fishman, Judy Aulette, Jerry Lembcke, Martha Gimenez, John Leggett, Bob Parker, Bill Domhoff, Julia Fox, Jan Fritz, David Dickens, Karl Kreplin, David L. Harvey, Lyle Warner, and Johnson Makoba for their contributions to discussions on various currents in classical and contemporary social theory.

I would like to thank Denise Schaar and Lisa Stowell for typing several chapters of this book, Irene Glynn for doing an excellent job in copyediting the manuscript, and Ravi Mehra, my publisher, for his exemplary professional work in every stage of the publication process.

This book is dedicated to my introductory sociology and social theory students, who have, over the years, urged me to undertake this project—a task that I gladly undertook to meet this need.

INTRODUCTION

The origins of modern social theory goes back to the classical Greek philosophers Aristotle, Socrates, and Plato, who had an important influence on subsequent generations of social theorists through the Enlightenment to the late nineteenth and early twentieth centuries. While great social thinkers like Jean Jacques Rousseau, who became one of the leading theorists of the Enlightenment, developed their ideas on the foundations of rationalist and empiricist modes of thought dominant in the seventeenth century, they also generated their own uniquely eighteenth-century concept of society and social relations by integrating into their social analysis the scientific discoveries of thinkers like Isaac Newton, who revolutionized the study of nature and set forth a new standard for scientific research.[1]

The intellectual climate of this period was further enhanced by the French Revolution, which brought an added optimism to the improvement of the human condition. These developments in the eighteenth century, however, led to the conservative reaction of the early nineteenth century and at the same time marked a shift in direction of social theory, ushering in the social thought of a new stream of theorists—David Hume, Immanuel Kant, Edmund Burke, and Georg Wilhelm Friedrich Hegel.[2]

The postrevolutionary period gave rise, above all, to the emergence not only of a conservative reaction—which, as in the theories of Louis de Bonald and Joseph de Maistre, advocated a return to the prerevolutionary medieval social order—but to two other strands of thought, one that adhered to the preservation of the existing order, as in the case of Auguste Comte, and another that went beyond the status quo in the direction of an egalitarian social order embracing what Karl Marx later called a form of "utopian socialism," as in the case of Henri Comte de Saint-Simon.[3] These two strands established, by the mid-nineteenth century, the conservative and liberal/radical paths that came to define the parameters of competing traditions in the formation of modern sociological theory. Thus,

1

whereas Comte's conservative theorizing led to the emergence of Durkheimian and later Parsonian sociology, Saint-Simon's intellectual challenge to the old order led to the bourgeois (Weberian) and proletarian (Marxist) modes of social thought that came to provide alternative liberal and radical interpretations of society.

The collective contributions to social theory of the great thinkers of past centuries evolved by the late nineteenth and early twentieth centuries into the alternative theoretical perspectives of Durkheim, Weber, and Marx, which most sociologists view as having marked a major turning point in classical social theory. These three intellectual giants developed their thinking in direct response to the great social transformations of the eighteenth and nineteenth centuries, a period when the full implications and consequences of life in capitalist society were becoming apparent in all their social, economic, and political dimensions.[4] It was Karl Marx who first developed a comprehensive analysis of the fundamental contradictions of capitalism and established the parameters of discussion and debate on the nature of society and the social order that others, among them Durkheim, Weber, Gaetano Mosca, Sigmund Freud, and George Herbert Mead, later came to address.[5] In fact, as Irving Zeitlin has pointed out in his *Ideology and the Development of Sociological Theory*, Marx's work provoked a response that accounts for much of the theoretical arguments developed by these and other social theorists of this period and prompted, as Zeitlin puts it, "the intense debate with his [Marx's] ghost," one that has shaped, "in a large measure, the character of Western sociology."[6]

Analysis of the various explanations given by classical social theorists concerning the nature of society and social relations provides us with an occasion to examine briefly three fundamentally different theoretical approaches, or what Thomas Kuhn has called paradigms,[7] in classical and contemporary social theory: (1) the organic approach; (2) the individualistic approach; and (3) the organizational approach.

The organic approach, adopted by Durkheim, emphasizes the study of social order. Society in this context is conceived as an organism functioning much as the human body, where the various parts making up the organism contribute to the maintenance of the organism as a whole. Thus, for the smooth functioning of society, each part making up the system must function in organic harmony with the whole. Social order, consensus, equilibrium, and maintenance of the status quo are the central questions taken up for study; and disorganization of the family structure, breakdown of the moral order (especially of religion), as well as the decline in traditional cultural values are social problems typically studied by this approach. Culture, tradition, and long-held social values, seen as the primary motive force of social life, define the source and logic of social relations within this conservative conception of society and the social order, where society is viewed as an entity greater than the individuals who comprise it.

The individualistic approach, which Weber adopted as a theoretical expression of the newly emergent capitalist social order, gives primacy to the individual as the motive force of social development. Based on the logic of competition, private enterprise, and individualism as the defining characteristics of the new society in the making, this approach concentrates on the individual as the unit of analysis, emphasizing the importance of such concepts as the actor, personality, the self, motivation, and adaptation. Although Weber and a few others in this tradition also addressed larger, structural phenomena, such as status, authority, and bureaucracy, the heavy reliance of this approach on human nature as the motive force of society and social relations gives this approach primarily a micro-level orientation, where problems affecting society are defined in terms of individual deviance, maladjustment, and other problems that can be solved only by the successful reintegration of the individual into the existing social order.

Finally, the organizational approach, articulated by Marx, emphasizes the centrality of social organization and focuses on class relations and class struggles as the motive force of social change and social transformation. This approach highlights the exploitation of labor as the most important, indeed the central, problematic of capitalist society—one that is based on class conflict and class struggles. The nature of society and the social order, as well as the position of individuals within it, are viewed in terms of the dominant mode of production determined by the social relations of production (or class relations), which define the parameters of the course and direction of broader social relations in society. Instead of the integration of the individual into the dominant culture and morality, as in the conservative organic position, or the adaptation of the individual into society through control of personal deviation from social norms, as in the liberal individualistic position, Marx's organizational approach contends that it is not the individual but society based on class inequalities, hence class conflict, that is the source of social tensions and instability. Thus, class struggles and struggles for political power are the collective expression of individuals adversely affected in society, individuals who eventually organize and struggle collectively to improve their situation and thereby advance their interests.

The political implications of the three approaches can be delineated rather clearly if one places them in their proper historical context. While all three schools of thought developed in direct response to the changing social, economic, and political conditions in the eighteenth and nineteenth centuries, these schools represented the interests of diverse classes that came to define the social context of a declining or ascending order in a most crucial period of epochal social transformation—the transition from feudalism to capitalism and the consolidation of capitalist rule in the nineteenth century.

The organic approach was a conservative reaction to the newly emergent capitalist order and advocated a return to the old feudal system, wherein society functioned around established traditional cultural precepts, where the church was supreme, and where the individual was bound to the moral values of the medieval order. Viewing the rising capitalist system as a formula for moral decadance and social decline, the proponents of the organic approach thus argued in favor of social cohesion and social solidarity, which they felt were characteristic of the old moral code.

The individualistic approach, in contrast, lent its support to the rising capitalist order wherein old traditions were giving way to individual self-advancement in a market-oriented economy founded on private ownership of the means of production, competition, and individualism. The individualistic school viewed the decline of the old order as a step forward in human freedom—freedom from bondage to the church or any other moral authority that dictated the terms of social life, and freedom to accumulate private capital in accordance with the laws of the market. Thus this approach was conducive to and in effect came to advance the interests of the capitalist class as against the feudal landlords on the one hand and the wage-earning working class on the other.

Finally, the organizational approach, while supportive of the limited human freedoms achieved under the new social order, criticized the amassing of wealth from private profit based on the exploitation of labor. Thus it threw its lot with the oppressed and exploited laboring masses it believed would eventually become conscious of their class interests and struggle for the abolition of private property and private profit through a revolutionary transformation of capitalist society, establishing in its place an egalitarian social order.

Durkheim, Weber, and Marx thus provided three alternative responses to the burning questions of their time and thereby established the parameters of these competing perspectives at the broader theoretical level. These approaches have come to play a central role in the development of social theory over the past century, incorporating the contributions of many of the social theorists included in this book, and are viewed by most sociologists today as representing the best elements of classical and contemporary social theory.[8]

This book is divided into two parts. Part I focuses on classical social theory and examines the works of thirteen social theorists of the late nineteenth and early twentieth centuries. Part II provides an analysis of the works of thirteen contemporary social theorists of the middle to late twentieth century. The book concludes with some reflections on the nature of social theory and its central role in critical intellectual discourse.

The theories examined in the chapters that make up this book present a sampling of the rich traditions of both classical and contemporary social theory. By providing an overview of the works of some of the most important theorists of the nineteenth and twentieth centuries, the book addresses a variety of controversial theoretical issues that have brought social theorizing to the forefront of critical analysis.

Notes

[1] Jean Jaques Rousseau, *The Social Contract* (New York: Dutton, 1950).

[2] See, for example, David Hume, *A Treatise of Human Nature* (Oxford: Claredon Press, 1949); Immanuel Kant, *Critique of Pure Reason* (New York: St. Martin's Press, 1929); Edmund Burke, *Reflections on the Revolution in France* (New Roch-

elle, N.Y.: Arlington House, n.d.); G.W.F. Hegel, *The Philosophy of History* (New York: Dover, 1956); and idem, *Science of Logic* (London: Allen and Unwin, 1969).

[3] Auguste Comte, *The Positive Philosophy*, 2 vols. (London: Kegan Paul, 1893); Henri de Saint-Simon, *Social Organization, the Science of Man and Other Writings* (New York: Harper and Row, 1964).

[4] For an excellent discussion of the changes taking place in Western Europe during this period, see Maurice Dobb, *Studies in the Development of Capitalism* (New York: International Publishers, 1963). See also Karl Polanyi, *The Great Transformation* (Boston: Beacon, 1957).

[5] See Karl Marx, *Capital*, 3 vols. (New York: International Publishers, 1967).

[6] Irving M. Zeitlin, *Ideology and the Development of Sociological Theory* (Englewood Cliffs, N.J.: Prentice Hall, 1968), viii.

[7] Thomas S. Kuhn, *The Structure of Scientific Revolutions*, 2nd ed. (Chicago: University of Chicago Press, 1970).

[8] See, for example, David L. Westby, *The Growth of Sociological Theory* (Englewood Cliffs, N.J.: Prentice Hall, 1991).

PART I

CLASSICAL SOCIAL THEORY

Chapter	**1**	**MARX AND ENGELS ON SOCIAL CLASS AND CLASS STRUGGLE**

Karl Marx (1818–83) and Frederick Engels (1820–95), the most prominent and controversial social theorists of the nineteenth century, provided an analysis of social classes and class struggles in society aimed at understanding the root causes of class inequality based on the exploitation of labor. The analysis of class structure, exploitation, and class struggle, they stressed, must be placed within the framework of the dynamics of social change in the world historical process. The crucial task for them, therefore, was to identify and examine the primary motive force of social transformation that defined the parameters of societal development: *class struggle*. Hence, to understand the centrality of class and class struggle in the Marxist analysis of society and social structure, we first briefly discuss the methodological foundation of the Marxist approach—dialectical and historical materialism.

Dialectical and Historical Materialism

The dialectical method, developed by G.W.F. Hegel, explains phenomena in terms of an endless process of transformation of contradictions resulting from the unity of opposites (i.e., thesis vs. antithesis leading to synthesis). Whereas Hegel applied the dialectical approach to the realm of *ideas* (i.e., the clash of ideas *A* and *B* giving rise to idea *C*), Marx and Engels adapted it to the realm of the material world to explain the interaction between ideas (theory) and social reality (practice). Going a step further, Marx and Engels transformed Hegel's dialectical idealism into their materialist dialectics by placing ideas in their social, material context. By applying it to the real world, they were able to explain the structure of social relations which, in class society, is based on the struggle between opposing *classes*.

9

Advancing their materialist conception of social reality, Marx and Engels argued that the material condition of human beings—their real-life experience, their social existence—determines their consciousness. Consequently, the social reality in which humans live molds their thought:

> The production of ideas, of conceptions, of consciousness is at first directly interwoven with the material activity and the material intercourse of men, the language of real life. Conceiving, thinking, the mental intercourse of men, appear at this stage as the direct efflux of their material behavior. The same applies to mental production as expressed in the language of the politics, laws, morality, religion, metaphysics of a people.[1]

Elsewhere, Marx states clearly that "it is not the consciousness of men that determines their being, but on the contrary, their social being that determines their consciousness."[2] Thus the material world is prior to and a necessary condition for the emergence of consciousness.

Criticizing Hegel's idealist conception of dialectics, Marx and Engels point out that

> in direct contrast to German philosophy which descends from heaven to earth, here we ascend from earth to heaven. That is to say, we do not set out from what men say, imagine, conceive, nor from men as narrated, thought of, imagined, conceived, in order to arrive at men in the flesh. We set out from real, active men, and on the basis of their real life-process we demonstrate the development of the ideological reflexes and echoes of this life-process.[3]

The starting point in Marx and Engels's analysis of society and social relations is the recognition of human beings as the prime agents of material production—a process that forms the basis of production and reproduction of human existence. As they put it:

> Life involves before everything else eating and drink-
> ing, a habitation, clothing and many other things. The
> first historical act is thus the production of the means to
> satisfy these needs, the production of material life
> itself.[4]

Hence, in the early stages of history, principal human needs were
based on and centered in subsistence for the sustenance of life.

Through time, humans created and developed tools, skills,
knowledge, and work habits—in short, the *forces of production*—to
an extent that permitted, for the first time, the accumulation of
surplus. Although in most of human history, for thousands of years,
human beings lived in classless primitive-communal societies, the
accumulation of a social surplus in the form of a surplus product
gave rise to the emergence of classes in society. With the development of social classes and class inequality, there emerged historically specific social *relations of production*, or class relations, between those who produced the surplus and those who claimed
ownership and control of that surplus (e.g., slaves vs. masters, serfs
vs. landlords, wage laborers vs. capitalists). Marx and Engels pointed
out that the forces of production (including the labor process at the
point of production) and the social relations of production (class
relations) together constitute a society's *mode of production*, or its
social-economic foundation, defined as the way in which a society's
wealth is produced and distributed—in short, the social-economic
system (e.g., slavery, feudalism, capitalism).

Applying these concepts to history and examining the material
conditions surrounding the production and reproduction process, in
effect the very basis of life itself, Marx and Engels observed that:

> The way in which men produce their means of subsis-
> tence depends first of all on the nature of the actual
> means they find in existence and have to reproduce.
> This mode of production must not be considered simply
> as being the reproduction of the physical existence of
> the individuals. Rather it is a definite form of activity of
> these individuals, a definite form of expressing their
> life, a definite *mode of life* on their part. As individuals
> express their life, so they are. What they are, therefore,

coincides with their production, both with *what* they produce and with *how* they produce. The nature of individuals thus depends on the material conditions determining their production.[5]

Engels, in a letter to Heinz Starkenburg, further explains the historical materialist outlook on society this way:

> What we understand by the economic conditions which we regard as the determining basis of the history of society are the methods by which human beings in a given society produce their means of subsistence and exchange the products among themselves (in so far as division of labour exists). Thus the *entire technique* of production and transport is here included. According to our conception this technique also determines the method of exchange and, further, the division of products and with it, after the dissolution of tribal society, the division into classes also and hence the relations of lordship and servitude and with them the state, politics, law, etc.[6]

Once a class society emerges—in which the production process is firmly established, a surplus is generated, and social classes have developed—the relations of production (or class relations) become the decisive element defining the nature of the dominant mode of production, which in turn gives rise to the political *superstructure*, including first and foremost the state, as well as other political and ideological institutions that serve the interests of the propertied classes in society. Thus the superstructure arises from and becomes a reflection of the dominant mode of production, which reinforces the existing social order, notwithstanding the fact that the superstructure itself may influence or otherwise effect changes in favor of the long-term interests of the dominant classes in society.[7] As Marx points out:

> In the social production of their life, men enter into definite relations that are indispensable and independent of their will, relations of production which correspond to a definite stage of development of their material

productive forces. The sum total of these relations of production constitutes the economic structure of society, the real foundation, on which rises a legal and political superstructure and to which correspond definite forms of social consciousness.[8]

For Marx, then, the *relations of production*, that is, the "relationship of the owners of the conditions of production to the direct producers," as he defines it, "reveals the innermost secret, the hidden basis of the entire social structure, and with it . . . the corresponding specific form of the state."[9] The relations of production, as the decisive element in the mode of production, together with the political superstructure that emerges from it, thus constitute the very basis of the analysis of social classes, class structure, class struggles, and social transformation, according to the Marxist classics.

Social Class and Class Struggle

The focal point stressed by Marx and Engels in explaining social class and class struggle is that an analysis of property-based unequal social relations prevalent in the organization of material production in class society is the key to an understanding of the nature of a particular social order. The position of people in the production process, situated according to their relation to the ownership/control of the means of production, is viewed by Marx and Engels as the decisive element defining class relations in society. It is from these historically-specific social relations of production that inequalities precisely arise and lead to class conflict and class struggles, that is, struggles for political power. Thus, refering to class society, "the history of all hitherto existing society," Marx and Engels point out, "is the history of class struggles."[10]

In capitalist society, for example, two main classes relate to one another in the production sphere: capitalists (owners of capital) and workers (wage labor). The capitalist class owns the means of production and accumulates capital through the exploitation of labor. The working class does not own the means of production but instead uses its labor power to generate value for the capitalists as a condition for its survival. As Marx and Engels point out, capitalist society is thus mainly divided into:

the class of modern capitalists, owners of the means of
social production and employers of wage-labor ... [and]
the class of modern wage-laborers who, having no
means of production of their own, are reduced to selling
their labor-power in order to live.[11]

Under capitalist production, while a portion of the value generated by labor is returned to it for subsistence (wages), a much greater
portion goes to the capitalist in the form of surplus value (profits),
which, accumulated over time, enhances the wealth and fortunes of
the capitalist class vis-à-vis all other classes in society, especially the
working class, in both relative and absolute terms.[12]

The accumulation of capital through this process of exploitation
under capitalism thus results in disparities in wealth and income
between labor and capital and eventually leads to conflict and
struggle between the two classes, extending to realms beyond the
production sphere itself. Hence, in this class struggle, write Marx
and Engels,

oppressor and oppressed stood in constant opposition to
one another, carried on an uninterrupted, now hidden,
now open fight, a fight that each time ended, either in a
revolutionary reconstitution of society at large, or in the
common ruin of the contending classes.[13]

Marx and Engels conceptualized class at three different yet
related levels: economic, social, and political. The first of these is
identified as the foundation of class analysis, class-in-itself (*Klasse-
an-sich*). This refers to groups of people who relate to production in
the same way, that is, those who have the same property relationships
in the productive process (e.g., workers, peasants, landlords, capitalists). Structurally, then, *class-in-itself* is the logical outcome of the
mode of production in all class societies.

At the next, sociological, level is what can be referred to as *social
class*. A class-in-itself becomes a social class only when there is a
close relationship between the members of a particular class. In this
sense, industrial workers (the classic proletariat) constitute a social
class in that not only do the members of this class interact in the
productive process (in factories, under socialized conditions of

production) but they also have a distinct culture, lifestyle, habits—
in short, a cohesive intraclass association, including intermarriage
between members of the same class.

Finally, the third and highest level of class is referred to by Marx
as that of class-for-itself (*Klasse-für-sich*). This means that a *Klasse-an-sich* that has become a social class has attained full consciousness of its interests and goals and engages in common political
activity in pursuit of its class interests.

Thus in capitalist society, the dominant capitalist class, through
its control of the major superstructural institutions, obtains political
control and disseminates ruling-class ideology, hence assuring its
ideological hegemony in society.

At the same time, to prevent the development of class consciousness among the masses and to neutralize and divert their
frustration and anger against the system, the dominant class facilitates the development of false consciousness among the working
class. This, in turn, serves to block the development of class
consciousness among workers and thus prevents, to the extent it is
successful, the potential for social revolution.

Nevertheless, the material conditions of life under capitalism
eventually incite workers to organize and rise up. As the working
class becomes class conscious and discovers that its social condition
is the result of its exploitation by the capitalists, it invariably begins
to organize and fight back to secure for itself economic benefits and
political rights denied in capitalist society—a society wherein the
exploitation of labor through the extraction of surplus value is
legally assured by the capitalist state.

This exploitation, hence domination, of the working class by
capital, Marx points out, would, sooner or later, lead to class
struggle, that is, a struggle for political power: "The conflict between
proletariat and bourgeoisie is a struggle of one class against another,
a struggle that means in its highest expression a total revolution."[14]
"Is there any reason to be surprised," Marx asks, "that a society
based on class conflict leads to brutal opposition, and in the last
resort to a clash between individuals?"[15] "An oppressed class," he
maintains, "is the condition of existence of every society based on
class conflict. Thus the liberation of the oppressed class necessarily
involves the creation of a new society," adding "only in an order of

things in which there are no class conflicts will social evolutions cease to be political revolutions."[16]

Political Power and the State

Political power, Marx and Engels point out, grows out of economic (class) power driven by money and wealth, but to maintain and secure their wealth, dominant classes of society establish and control political institutions to hold down the masses and assure their continued domination. The supreme superstructural institution that historically has emerged to carry out this task is the state.

The emergence of the state coincided with the emergence of social classes and class struggles resulting from the transition from a primitive communal to more advanced modes of production when an economic surplus was first generated. Ensuing struggles over control of this surplus led to the development of the state; once captured by the dominant classes in society, the state became an instrument of force to maintain the rule of wealth and privilege against the laboring masses, to maintain exploitation and domination by the few over the many. Without the development of such a powerful instrument of force, there could be no assurance of protection of the privileges of a ruling class, who clearly lived off the labor of the masses. The newly wealthy needed a mechanism that

> would not only safeguard the newly-acquired property
> of private individuals against the communistic traditions
> of the gentile order, would not only sanctify private
> property, formerly held in such light esteem, and pro-
> nounce this sanctification the highest purpose of human
> society, but would also stamp the gradually developing
> new forms of acquiring property, and consequently, of
> constantly accelerating increase in wealth, with the seal
> of general public recognition; an institution that would
> perpetuate, not only the newly-rising class division of
> society, but also the right of the possessing class to
> exploit the non-possessing classes and the rule of the
> former over the latter.

> And this institution arrived. The *state* was in-
> vented.[17]

Thus the state developed as an institution as a result of the growth of wealth and social classes:

> Former society, moving in class antagonisms, had need
> of the state, that is, an organization of the exploiting
> class at each period for the maintenance of its external
> conditions of production; that is, therefore, for the
> forcible holding down of the exploited class in the
> conditions of oppression (slavery, villeinage or serfdom,
> wage labor) determined by the existing mode of pro-
> duction. The state was the official representative of
> society as a whole, its embodiment in a visible corpo-
> ration; but it was this only in so far as it was the state of
> that class which itself, in its epoch, represented society
> as a whole; in ancient times, the state of the slave-
> owning citizens; in the Middle Ages, of the feudal
> nobility; in our epoch, of the bourgeoisie.[18]

In *The Origins of the Family, Private Property and the State*, Engels writes:

> It is, as a rule, the state of the most powerful, economically
> dominant class, which, through the medium of the state,
> becomes also the politically dominant class, and thus
> acquires new means of holding down and exploiting the
> oppressed class. Thus, the state of antiquity was above
> all the state of the slave owners for the purpose of
> holding down the slaves, as the feudal state was the
> organ of the nobility for holding down the peasant serfs
> and bondsmen, and the modern representative state is an
> instrument of exploitation of wage labor by capital.[19]

Thus, in all class-divided societies throughout history, "political power is merely the organized power of one class for oppressing another."[20]

In modern capitalist society, the state, reflecting the interests of the dominant capitalist class, can thus be identified as the *capitalist state*, for as Marx and Engels point out, this state is nothing more than a political organ of the bourgeoisie adopted for the "guarantee of their property and interests."[21] Hence, "the bourgeoisie has . . . conquered for itself, in the modern representative State, exclusive political sway. The executive of the modern State is but a committee for managing the common affairs of the whole bourgeoisie."[22] In this sense, the struggle of the working class against capital takes on both an economic *and* a political content:

> The more it [the state] becomes the organ of a particular class, the more it directly enforces the supremacy of that class. The fight of the oppressed class against the ruling class becomes necessarily a political fight, a fight first of all against the political dominance of this class.[23]

Seen in this context, the centrality of the state as an instrument of *class rule* takes on an added importance in the analysis of social class and class struggles, for political power contested by the warring classes takes on its real meaning in securing the rule of the victorious class when that power is ultimately exercised through the instrumentality of the state.

Conclusion

We have seen that for Marx and Engels the concepts of social class and class struggle are central to their analysis of society and social relations. Moreover, their interest in class structure is a result of their larger quest to understand the dynamics of social change and social transformation within the world historical process. In this context, their understanding of the motive force of historical progress and the agents of societal change have brought to the fore the question of political power and the state. Thus, Marx and Engels's focus on production relations, informing their concept of social class, exploitation, and class struggle, as the foundation of the historical materialist conception of society and social life, including the role of the state and power relations in society, makes an important contribution to classical social theory as well as to our understanding of class structure in modern society. In fact, as we see in subsequent chapters, many of the prominent social theorists of the late nineteenth and much of the twentieth century were either influenced by the theories of Marx and Engels or developed their own theories in direct opposition to those of the Marxist classics.

Notes

[1] Karl Marx and Frederick Engels, *The German Ideology* (New York: International Publishers, 1947), 13-14.

[2] Karl Marx, "Preface to *A Contribution to the Critique of Political Economy*," in K. Marx and F. Engels, *Selected Works* (New York: International Publishers, 1972), 182.

[3] Marx and Engels, *German Ideology*, 14.

[4] Ibid., 16.

[5] Ibid., 7.

[6] Frederick Engels, "Letter to Heinz Starkenburg" in K. Marx and F. Engels, *Selected Correspondence* (New York: International Publishers, 1935), 516.

[7] See Marx and Engels, *German Ideology*; Karl Marx, *The Poverty of Philosophy* (New York: International Publishers, 1963); Marx, "Preface to *A Contribution to a Critique of Political Economy*,"; Karl Marx, *Capital*, vol. 3 (Moscow: Foreign Languages Publishing House, 1962); Frederick Engels, *Anti-Duhring* (New York: International Publishers, 1976), pt. 2; and other writings of Marx and Engels.

[8] Marx, "Preface to *A Contribution to a Critique of Political Economy*," 182.

[9] Marx, *Capital*, 3:772.

[10] Karl Marx and Frederick Engels, "Manifesto of the Communist Party," in Marx and Engels, *Selected Works*, 35.

[11] Ibid.

[12] Surplus value (or gross profits) is that part of the total value created by labor that workers surrender to the owners of the means of production after receiving only a small portion of the total value in the form of wages. Although the end result is the same, the extraction of surplus value from the producers takes on different forms in social formations dominated by different, historically-specific mode(s) of production.

[13] Marx and Engels, "Manifesto," 36.

[14] Marx quoted in Ralph Dahrendorf, *Class and Class Conflict in Industrial Society* (Stanford: Stanford University Press, 1959), 18.

[15] Ibid.

[16] Ibid.

[17] Frederick Engels, *The Origin of the Family, Private Property and the State* (New York: International Publishers, 1972), 263.

[18] Engels, *Anti-Duhring*, 306.

[19] Engels, *The Origin*.

[20] Marx and Engels, "Manifesto", 53.

[21] Marx and Engels, *German Ideology*, 59.

[22] Marx and Engels, "Manifesto", 37.

[23] Frederick Engels, "Ludwig Feuerbach and the End of Classical German Philosophy," in Marx and Engels, *Selected Works*, 627.

Chapter	**2**	**DURKHEIM ON SOCIETY** **AND THE SOCIAL ORDER**

Emile Durkheim (1858–1917), one of the eminent social theorists of the late nineteenth and early twentieth centuries, has with a select few other theorists shared center stage in classical sociological theory during the past century. Together with the two other giants of classical social theory—Karl Marx and Max Weber—Durkheim has left his mark in sociology as one of the great social thinkers of our time.

This chapter examines the major ideas set forth by Durkheim concerning human nature, society, and the social order. Limited in scope, our analysis focuses on Durkheim's attempt to develop an organic theory of society.[1]

Human Nature

Durkheim, in advancing his sociological critique of Western industrial society and its impact on the quality of individual and social life, made a number of key assumptions about human nature that were fundamentally different from and opposed to those of Marx and Engels. Thus, to understand Durkheim and his theory of society and social structure, we must first understand his underlying assumptions about human nature.

"Our first duty," writes Durkheim in his major work *The Division of Labor in Society*, "is to make a moral code for ourselves."[2] This moral code is crucial, he argues, because it constitutes the very foundation of social solidarity:

> [Moral] discipline . . . is a code of rules that lays down for the individual what he should do so as not to damage collective interests and so as not to disorganize the society of which he forms a part. . . . It is this discipline

that curbs him, that marks the boundaries, that tells him
what his relations with his associates should be, where
illicit encroachments begin, and what he must pay in
current dues towards the maintenance of the community.[3]

But why does Durkheim suggest that we need such a system of
social control? Further, why is it "necessary" that the creative
expression of individuals be curbed? "The interests of the individual," writes Durkheim, "are not those of the group he belongs to
and indeed there is often a real antagonism between the one and the
other."[4] Moreover,

these social interests that the individual has to take into
account are only dimly perceived by him: sometimes he
fails to perceive them at all, because . . . he is not
constantly aware of them, as he is of all that concerns
and interests himself. It seems, then, that there should be
some system which brings them to mind, which obliges
him to respect them, and this system can be no other than
a moral discipline.[5]

Durkheim's argument here is both basic and simple: To promote
and advance the larger (social) interests of the group and to limit
excessive self-interest, the individual must be guided by a "moral
code" that implants such values throughout society. To be effective,
the adoption of a "moral discipline," he stresses, must take place
during early childhood socialization. Durkheim makes this point
quite clear when he says:

Education must help the child understand at an early
point that, beyond certain contrived boundaries that
constitute the historical framework of justice, there are
limits based on the nature of things, that is to say, in the
nature of each of us. This has nothing to do with
insidiously inculcating a spirit of resignation in the
child; or curbing his legitimate ambitions; or preventing
him from seeing the conditions existing around him.
Such proposals would contradict the very principles of

everything essential in the relations which are to be explained: for it is an eternal truth that outside of us there exists something greater than us, with which we enter into communion.

That is why we can rest assured in advance that the practices of the cult, whatever they may be, are something more than movements without importance and gestures without efficacy. By the mere fact that their apparent function is to strengthen the bonds attaching the believer to his god, they at the same time really strengthen the bonds attaching the individual to the society of which he is a member, since the god is only a figurative expression of the society.[20]

Thus, in Durkheim's language, the functions of "religion," "god," and "society" become one and the same: They all represent forces of integration, cohesion, conformity, and, in the final analysis, *order* in society. Here, once again, we see another of Durkheim's repeated attempts to reify society: Society, he writes,

has the chief interest in order and peace; if anomie is an evil, it is above all because society suffers from it, being unable to live without cohesion and regularity. A moral or juridical regulation essentially expresses, then, social needs that society alone can feel.[21]

Thus Durkheim tells us that to maintain harmony between individuals and between them and their society, what is needed is a strong sense of social solidarity.

In *The Division of Labor in Society* Durkheim discusses two kinds of solidarity: (1) mechanical and (2) organic. Mechanical solidarity is based on "states of conscience which are common to all the members of the same society."[22] Thus it is rooted in likenesses and collective sentiments. "Solidarity which comes from likenesses," writes Durkheim, "is at its maximum when the collective conscience completely envelops our whole conscience and coincides in all its points with it."[23] To clarify the nature of this type of solidarity further, Durkheim points out that "at the moment this solidarity exercises its force, our personality vanishes, as our definition permits us to say, for we are no longer ourselves, but the collective life."[24]

What Durkheim is pointing to in this passage is the conflict between the collective conscience and the individual. How can this conflict be resolved within the framework of mechanical solidarity? It can be resolved, according to Durkheim, only by moving to a higher level of solidarity, that which he calls "organic." And the division of labor is the mechanism that raises society to that higher level. Thus the division of labor plays a positive role and becomes the principal social bond among the members of advanced societies, one that reconciles the interests of both the individual and society. Durkheim writes:

> Since mechanical solidarity progressively becomes enfeebled, life properly social must decrease or another solidarity must slowly come in to take the place of that which has gone. The choice must be made. In vain shall we contend that the collective conscience extends and grows stronger at the same time as that of individuals. . . . Social progress, however, does not consist in a continual dissolution. On the contrary, the more we advance, the more profoundly do societies reveal the sentiment of self and of unity. There must, then, be some other social link which produces this result; this cannot be any other than that which comes from the division of labor. . . . It is the division of labor which, more and more, fills the role that was formerly filled by the common conscience. It is the principal bond of social aggregates of higher types.[25]

In Durkheim's view, then, the division of labor—the specialization of societal functions—brings about two important developments: (1) it enhances one's individuality through detachment from the "common conscience," while (2) it assures a higher level of social solidarity as a result of the assignment of specific functions to individual members of society.

Conclusion

This chapter has attempted to present a brief statement of Durkheim's views concerning human nature and society. And in the process of our analysis we have examined his major theoretical positions regarding society and the social order, developed as a response to the harsh realities of social life under capitalism in the late nineteenth and early twentieth centuries—a response that represents a clear statement of an ideological position transformed into a conservative social theory that Durkheim attempted to develop in order to contribute to the remedy of problems engendered by emergent industrial capitalism. Although his critique of early capitalist society is laden with attempts to develop a new morality to maintain order in society—hence in this sense it has conservative political implications—his analysis of the dynamics of society and the social order during this period has broader significance with regard to its overall contribution to classical social theory.

Notes

[1] See, for example, Robert N. Bellah, "Durkheim and History," *American Sociological Review* 24, no. 4 (August 1959): 447–60; Anthony Giddens, *Capitalism and Modern Social Theory* (New York: Cambridge University Press, 1971); Kurt H. Wolff, ed., *Emile Durkheim, 1858–1917*, (Columbus, Ohio: Ohio State University Press, 1960).

[2] Emile Durkheim, *The Division of Labor in Society* (New York: Free Press, 1964), 409.

[3] Emile Durkheim, *Professional Ethics and Civic Morals* (Glencoe, Ill.: Free Press, 1958), 14–15.

[4] Ibid., 14.

[5] Ibid.

[6] Emile Durkheim, *Moral Education* (New York: Free Press of Glencoe, 1961), 49.

[7] Ibid., 43.

[8] Emile Durkheim, *Suicide: A Study in Sociology* (New York: Free Press, 1951), 210.

[9] Ibid., 373.

[10] Ibid.

[11] We assume here that Durkheim means *any* society, including the exploitative capitalist society in which he himself lived.

[12] Durkheim, *Suicide*, 254.

[13] As, for example, with regard to slaves in slaveowning societies and workers in capitalist society, to cite only two cases that raise serious questions about an approach that plays a legitimizing role vis-à-vis the maintenance of order in society.

[14] Durkheim, *Suicide*, 38.

[15] James W. Russell, *Introduction to Macrosociology* (Englewood Cliffs, N.J.: Prentice Hall, 1992), 90–91.

[16] Emile Durkheim, *The Rules of the Sociological Method* (New York: Free Press, 1964), 123.

[17] Durkheim, *Suicide*, 38–39.

[18] Emile Durkheim, *Education and Sociology* (Glencoe, Ill.: Free Press, 1956), 76.

[19] Emile Durkheim, *The Elementary Forms of Religious Life* (London: Allen & Unwin, 1957), 225.

[20] Ibid., 225–26.

[21] Durkheim, *The Division of Labor in Society*, 5.

[22] Ibid., 109.

[23] Ibid., 130.

[24] Ibid.

[25] Ibid., 173.

	3	**WEBER ON BUREAUCRACY,**
Chapter		**POWER, AND SOCIAL STATUS**

Max Weber (1864–1920) is considered by many to be one of the greatest social theorists of the late nineteenth and early twentieth centuries. While he was influenced by the great social thinkers of his period, Weber developed a distinct approach to the analysis of the state, bureaucracy, and power—an approach that constitutes an alternative to both Durkheimian and Marxist conceptions of power, politics, and society.[1]

This chapter focuses on Weber's theory of bureaucracy, power, class, and status and provides us with an analysis of their relationship in developing an understanding of the Weberian approach to the study of society.

Bureaucracy

What distinguishes Weber's analysis of bureaucracy from that of Marx and lends itself to an affinity with classical elite theory is his attempt to assign a *quasi*-autonomous role to the state wherein the bureaucrats appear to be serving their own interests, and the bureaucracy appears to be a power unto itself, with more and more permanent features. Operating at this secondary, institutional level, "bureaucracy," writes Weber, "is a power instrument of the first order," and adds that "where the bureaucratization of administration has been completely carried through, a form of power relation is established that is practically unshatterable."[2]

In Weber's view, bureaucracies are large-scale, impersonal organizations in which power relations are organized in a top-down hierarchical manner for purposes of efficiently attaining centrally defined goals. Thus bureaucratic discipline "is nothing but the consistently rationalized, methodically prepared and exact execution of the received order, in which all personal criticism is un-

31

conditionally suspended and the actor is unswervingly and exclusively set for carrying out the command."[3]

"The decisive reason for the advance of bureaucratic organization," Weber writes, "has always been its purely *technical* superiority over any other form of organization."[4]

> The fully developed bureaucratic apparatus compares with other organizations exactly as does the machine with the non-mechanical modes of production. Precision, speed, unambiguity, knowledge of the files, continuity, discretion, unity, strict subordination, reduction of friction and of material and personal costs—these are raised to the optimum point in the strictly bureaucratic administration, and especially in its monocratic form.[5]

Outlining Weber's description of the general characteristics of a bureaucratic administrative staff, David L. Westby provides a summary list of the structural features of bureaucratic organization and the characteristics of bureaucratic officialdom as follows:

A. *Organizational features:*

1. Official jurisdictional areas ordered by rules, so that organizational activities are assigned as official duties delimited in a stable way by rules and continuously fulfilled.

2. An established hierarchy of authority under a central authority.

3. Separation of office from private domicile and performance of organizational duties on the basis of written documents maintained in files.

4. Office management presupposes specialized training as the basis for employment.

5. Organizational activities become full-time.

6. Management proceeds according to general rules, the knowledge of which "represents a special technical expertise."

B. *Characteristics of officialdom:*

1. The holding of office is a vocation, meaning that incumbency is based on training and evidence of competence, and that the official is oriented to discharge of office as a "duty."

2. There is a strong relationship between certain organizational characteristics and the extent to which office incumbency determines the status position of the official.

3. The official is appointed.

4. Tenure tends to be for life. This has the effect of contributing to the performance of the organization, but may affect the social status of the official and the technical efficiency of the organization negatively.

5. The official is remunerated by a money salary (and so a money economy is a presupposition of a bureaucracy).

6. The official moves through a career within the organizational hierarchy. This, along with (4) and (5) contributes to the creation of office sinecures in the form of prebends.[6]

In this context of the nature of bureaucratic administration, Weber notes the rise to prominence of the "expert" as a logical outcome of the growth of society and of bureaucracy: "The more complicated and specialized modern culture becomes, the more its external supporting apparatus demands the personally detached and strictly objective expert."[7] Through the possession of technical knowledge, the expert is able to obtain "a position of extraordinary power." Moreover, "bureaucratic organizations, or the holders of power who make use of them," Weber continues, "have the tendency to increase their power still further by the knowledge growing out of experience in the service."[8] But "expertise alone does not explain the power of bureaucracy"; equally important is the bureaucrats' possession of "official information" to which they and they alone have direct access—something that Weber sees as the "supreme power instrument" of the bureaucracy.[9]

The bureaucratic form of social organization, Weber argues, thus lends itself to control and domination of society and the individuals within it and generates as a by-product a social alienation that puts managers and workers, bureaucrats and citizens, in opposite camps, thus leading to conflict between those who control and govern and those who are controlled and governed at all levels of society.

Given their logic and organizational structure, bureaucracies, Weber believed, often take on lives of their own, which are often beyond the control of individual bureaucrats who take part in their daily operation. Thus, according to Weber, once a bureaucracy is firmly in place, it becomes a political force that can very seldom be successfully dismantled or eliminated.

> The individual bureaucrat cannot squirm out of the apparatus into which he has been harnessed. . . . In the great majority of cases he is only a small cog in a ceaselessly moving mechanism which prescribes to him an essentially fixed route of march. . . .
>
> The ruled, for their part, cannot dispense with or replace the bureaucratic apparatus once it exists. . . . Increasingly the material fate of the masses depends upon the continuous and correct functioning of the ever more bureaucratic organizations of private capitalism, and the idea of eliminating them becomes more and more utopian.[10]

The key question then becomes one of determining *who* controls and directs the complex bureaucratic machine. Unlike Robert Michels, Weber does *not* believe bureaucracy is, in essence, an autonomous power unto itself; rather, it is a tool or instrument *of* power:

> The bureaucratic structure goes hand in hand with the concentration of the material means of management in the hands of the master. This concentration occurs, for instance, in a well-known and typical fashion in the development of big capitalist enterprises, which find their essential characteristics in this process. A corresponding process occurs in public organizations.[11]

Thus, "the consequences of bureaucracy," Weber concludes, "depend therefore upon the direction which *the powers using the apparatus* give to it."[12] Weber's statement here could be interpreted in two possible ways: one that assigns primacy to the *political* process and grants a special role to the bureaucrats—as individuals and as a group—who manage the day-to-day affairs of the political apparatus, and another where the source of power is located outside the narrow confines of the political institutions in which individual bureaucrats and the bureaucracy as a whole operate—that is, the economy and class structure of society.

It is not surprising that most contemporary Weberians have separated Weber's analysis of bureaucracy from his generalized theory of class and power in society and thus have managed to give a conservative twist to his otherwise controversial analysis. Viewed within a broader societal context, however, it becomes clear that bureaucracy and political power to Weber are the manifestations of the real social forces that dominate the social-economic structure of modern society. Thus, to give primacy to the analytic strength of these secondary political concepts would mean one is dealing with surface phenomena. This is clearly evident, for example, in the works of most contemporary theorists of complex organizations, where power is consistently located within the structure of specific bureaucratic organizations, while bureaucracies are given a logic of their own and are conceived in terms of their special power and dynamics. But, to Weber, to understand more fully the logic of bureaucracy and political control one must examine the nature of property, income, status, and other dimensions of class relations, in society. It is here, in his differential conceptualization of class, status, and power based on market relations that one finds a uniquely Weberian approach in classical social theory.

Class, Status, and Power

It is often pointed out by the proponents of the Weberian approach that Weber's theory of stratification and inequality is "multidimensional." By this is meant that Weber utilized a number of equally important concepts to explain social structure and social inequality. The key variables in his conceptual scheme are class, status, and power.

To Weber, "a 'class' is any group of persons occupying the same class status" or situation.[13] "We may speak of a 'class,'" he writes, "when (1) a number of people have in common a specific causal component of their life chances, in so far as (2) this component is represented exclusively by economic interests in the possession of goods and opportunities for income, and (3) is represented under the conditions of the commodity or labor markets."[14] Central to Weber's conceptualization of class is the notion of "life chances," by which he means "the kind of control or lack of it which the individual has over goods or services and existing possibilities of their exploitation for the attainment of receipts within a given economic order."[15]

In the Weberian formulation of class, "class situation" is ultimately "market situation": "According to our terminology," writes Weber, "the factor that creates 'class' is unambiguously economic interest, and indeed, only those interests involved in the existence of the 'market.'"[16]

One's "class situation," then, is expressed by one's access to "a supply of goods, external living conditions, and personal life experiences"—all of which are derivative of and determined by the amount of control one has and which is exercised in the acquisition of income within a particular economic order. And at the center of this control lies, according to Weber, the key (economic) variable "property."

"'Property' and 'lack of property,'" argues Weber, are "the basic categories of all class situations."[17] In this formulation, one's life chances are "primarily determined by the differentiation of property holdings" and power is derived from the ownership and control of property "which gives [the owners] a monopoly to acquire [highly valued] goods."[18] And since the specific life chances of individuals is created by "the way in which the disposition over material property is distributed, . . . this mode of distribution monopolizes the opportunities for profitable deals for all those who [possess property]."[19]

Although Weber's conception of "property" is somewhat different than the Marxist definition, and that consequently such conception necessarily alters the analytical boundaries of the Weberian definition of the nature, position, and politics of specific classes, it does nonetheless point to the centrality of property relations in the control and execution of power in society.[20]

In addition to the "property class," which constitutes the determinant core of Weber's class analysis, Weber distinguishes two other classes that make up the totality of his class concepts: "acquisition class" and "social class."[21]

A class is an "acquisition class" when the class situation of its members is primarily determined by their opportunity for the exploitation of services on the market; the "social class" structure is composed of the plurality of class statuses between which an interchange of individuals on a personal basis or in the course of generations is readily possible and typically observable.[22]

While "acquisition classes" are based on occupational criteria, as opposed to property ownership, "social classes" are largely a product of the combination of occupational *and* property classes: the "working" class, the "lower middle" classes, the "intelligentsia," and "the classes occupying a privileged position through property and education."[23]

We cannot here go into a detailed description of each one of these classes, but suffice it to say that Weber, both in the case of property and acquisition classes, further subdivides them into "positively privileged" and "negatively privileged" classes and adds an intermediate category, making up the "middle class." As Weber puts it:

> Positively privileged property classes typically live from property income. This may be derived from property rights in human beings as with slaveowners, inland, in mining property, in fixed equipment such as plant and apparatus, in ships, and as creditors in loan relationships. . . . Finally, they may live on income from securities.
>
> Class interests which are negatively privileged with respect to property . . . are themselves objects of ownership, that is they are unfree [such as slaves].[24]

Although monopoly control over goods, services, wealth, education, high official position, income, accumulated surplus, and other privileges in the hands of the "positively privileged" property class and lack of such control and appropriation on the part of the "negatively privileged" property class place Weber's analytic scheme in a position that is in a sense analogous to the Marxist conception of exploiting and exploited classes, the logic of such classification is based on an entirely different set of conceptual definitions that separate the two traditions.[25]

"Social status" and "power" are two other major variables in the Weberian theoretical scheme, and we examine them briefly. "Social status," according to Weber, rests on "a typically effective claim to positive or negative privilege with respect to social prestige" derived from "one or more of the following bases: *(a)* mode of living, *(b)* a formal process of education . . . and the acquisition of the corresponding, modes of life, or *(c)* on the prestige of birth, or of an occupation."[26] Thus, within this framework, a social "*stratum*," then, "is a plurality of individuals who, within a larger group, enjoy a particular kind and level of prestige by virtue of their position."[27] As Weber puts it elsewhere:

> One might thus say that "classes" are stratified according to their relations to the production and acquisition of goods; whereas "status groups" are stratified according to the principles of their *consumption* of goods as represented by special "styles of life."[28]

And, as it is clear from Weber's repeated emphasis throughout his writings, *social status* is a manifestation of class situation, rooted in property relations, and thus is a derivative of *class* status.

Finally, the third major concept that is central to the Weberian theoretical scheme is "power." "In general, we understand by 'power,'" writes Weber, "the chance of a man or of a number of men to realize their own will in a communal action even against the resistance of others who are participating in the action."[29] Hence, although economic power is the single most important determinant of power as such, it may itself "be the consequence of power existing on other grounds." What is more, "power, including economic power, may be valued 'for its own sake.'" And, "very frequently the striving for power is also conditioned by the social 'honor' it entails."[30] "Indeed," adds Weber, "social honor, or prestige, may even be the basis of political or economic power, and very frequently has been."[31] But, nonetheless, viewed in its ultimate totality, it is economic power based on property ownership that is the crucial determinant of all power in society, according to Weber.

Conclusion

So, what do we make of Weber's position on bureaucracy, stratification, and class inequality? And what is the relationship between his key concepts, bureaucracy, class, status, and power, vis-à-vis the social collectivity? As we have previously noted and as the implications of the foregoing analysis make sufficiently clear, although Weber viewed these concepts as being relatively independent of one another, he did, nonetheless, stress that, in the final analysis, bureaucratic control, social status, and political power are dependent on and determined by *class*, that is, economic power.

On another level, Weber attempted to deal with a specific manifestation of economic power, namely, power accumulated and exercised at the administrative level of large organizations. He observed that the (vertical) means of administration of large organizations were becoming the dominant fact in all branches of modern society, and the type of organization becoming predominant was the bureaucracy. To be able to sort out clearly the source and linkages of power as it pertains to bureaucratic control, however, it is within the context of Weber's analysis of class structure that his position on bureaucracy must be understood. Framed in this way, we can more clearly comprehend the relationship between bureaucracy, class, power, and property in Weber's theory of modern society— one which has made a great contribution to classical social theory.

Notes

[1] The relationship between the economy, the state, religion and other spheres of social life are discussed by Weber in his early (1905) work *The Protestant Ethic and the Spirit of Capitalism* (New York: Scribners, 1948). Here Weber examines the relationship between Protestantism and the rise of capitalism and concludes that Protestantism played a key role in facilitating the development of capitalism in directly challenging the feudal system prevalent under medieval Catholicism in Europe during this period.

[2] Max Weber, *From Max Weber, Essays in Sociology*, trans., ed., and with an intro. by H.H. Gerth and C. Wright Mills (New York: Oxford University Press, 1967), 228.

[3] Max Weber, *Economy and Society*, 3 vols., ed. Guenther Roth and Claus Wittich (New York: Bedminster Press, 1968), 3:1149.

[4] Ibid., 973.

[5] Ibid.

[6] David L. Westby, *The Growth of Sociological Theory* (Englewood Cliffs, N.J.: Prentice Hall, 1991), 430. For an extended discussion of the characteristics of bureaucratic administration and staff, see Weber, *Economy and Society*, 3:956–63.

[7] Ibid., 975.

[8] Ibid., 1:225.

[9] Ibid., 3:1418.

[10] Ibid., 987–88.

[11] Ibid., 980.

[12] Weber, *From Max Weber*, 230; emphasis added.

[13] Max Weber, *The Theory of Social and Economic Organization*, ed. and with an intro. by Talcott Parsons (New York: Free Press, 1964), 424.

[14] Weber, *From Max Weber*, 181.

[15] Weber, *The Theory of Social and Economic Organization*, 424.

[16] Weber, *From Max Weber*, 183.

[17] Ibid., 182.

[18] Ibid.

[19] Ibid., 181–82.

[20] See Weber, *The Protestant Ethic and the Spirit of Capitalism*. As we have pointed out earlier, in the Weberian approach classes, including "property classes," are defined in terms of one's "market situation," whereas in Marxist theory class relations are based on social relations of production. See chapter 1 above.

[21] Weber, *The Theory of Social and Economic Organization*, 424.

[22] Ibid.

[23] Ibid., 427.

[24] Ibid., 425.

[25] For further discussion on this point, see chapter 1.

[26] Weber, *The Theory of Social and Economic Organization*, 428.

[27] Ibid., 428–29.

[28] Weber, *From Max Weber*, 193; emphasis in the original.

[29] Ibid., 180.

[30] Ibid.

[31] Ibid.

Chapter	**4**	**PARETO, MOSCA, AND MICHELS ON ELITES AND MASSES**

This chapter focuses on the political theories of three influential classical social theorists of the early twentieth century: Vilfredo Pareto, Gaetano Mosca, and Robert Michels. Together their work on elite formation and oligarchic rule constitutes the core of the classical bureaucratic elite theory of politics.

Classical elite theory maintains that all societies are ruled by elites and that the state is the political instrument by which the vast majority is ruled. This is so, according to this view, because the masses are inherently incapable of governing themselves; therefore, society must be led by a small number of individuals (the elite) who rule on behalf of the masses.

Elites and Their Circulation

In his major work, *The Mind and Society*, Vilfredo Pareto (1848–1923) set out to identify a minority of highly talented individuals at the top levels of society who possessed superior personal qualities and wielded great social and political power; distinguishing this group from the great masses of the people, Pareto called it the "*élite*".[1] "So let us make a class of the people who have the highest indices in their branch of activity," wrote Pareto, "and to that class give the name of *élite*."[2] Further elaborating on the internal composition of this group, he divided the elite into two (political and social) segments:

> A *governing élite*, comprising individuals who directly or indirectly play some considerable part in government, and a *non-governing élite*, comprising the rest. . . .
>
> So we get two strata in a population: (1) a lower stratum, the *non-élite*, with whose possible influence on

41

government we are not just here concerned; then (2) a
higher stratum, *the élite*, which is divided into two: *(a)*
a governing *élite*, *(b)* a non-governing *élite*.[3]

Within this framework, the fundamental idea set forth and
developed by Pareto was that of the "circulation of elites." By this,
Pareto meant two diverse processes operative in the perpetual
continuity of elite rule: (1) the process in which *individuals* circulate
between the elite and the nonelite; and (2) the process in which a
whole elite is replaced by a new one.

The main point of Pareto's concept of the circulation of elites is
that the ongoing process of replenishment of the governing elite by
superior individuals from the lower classes is a critical element
securing the continuation of elite rule.

> The governing class is restored not only in numbers,
> but—and that is the more important thing—in quality,
> by families rising from the lower classes and bringing
> with them the vigor and the proportions of residues
> necessary for keeping themselves in power.[4]

A breakdown in this process of circulation of elites, however,
leads to such serious instability in the social equilibrium that "the
governing class crashes to ruin and often sweeps the whole of a
nation along with it."[5]

In Pareto's reasoning, a "potent cause of disturbance in the
equilibrium is the accumulation of superior elements in the lower
classes and, conversely, of inferior elements in the higher classes."[6]
Hence, "every *élite* that is not ready to fight to defend its position is
in full decadence; there remains nothing for it to do but to vacate its
place for another *élite* having the verile qualities which it lacks."[7]

Thus, Pareto reaches an inescapable conclusion in his four-
volume study: "Aristocracies do not last. Whatever the causes, it is
an incontestable fact that after a certain length of time they pass
away. History is a graveyard of aristocracies."[8]

The consequences of developments in society are such that they
eventually lead to total social transformation, according to Pareto.
"Revolutions," he writes,

come about through accumulations in the higher strata of society ... of decadent elements no longer possessing the residues suitable for keeping them in power, and shrinking from the use of force; while meantime in the lower strata of society elements of superior quality are coming to the fore, possessing residues suitable for exercising the functions of government and willing enough to use force.[9]

Pareto's explanation of the nature and dynamics of elite rule and their circulation, therefore, rests in large part on the personal qualities of individuals in both elite and nonelite segments of society and their willingness or failure to use force to acquire and retain political power.

Pareto's concern with the decline in legitimacy of the existing order in Italy in the early decades of this century, together with the rising popularity of Marxism which he opposed, drove him to fascism. "Fascism, for Pareto," writes Irving Zeitlin,

seemed not only to confirm his theories but also to hold out hope for a "new era." That he identified with the new order is borne out by the fact that on March 23, 1923, he accepted an appointment as senator—a position he had declined to accept in the pre-fascist government. In a letter to an acquaintance at the time of acceptance, he wrote: "I am happy to see that you are favorably disposed to the new regime, which, in my opinion, is the only one capable of saving Italy from innumerable evils." And, in the same vein, "France will save herself only if she finds her own Mussolini."[10]

"In general," Zeitlin continues, "Pareto's attitude seems to have been that since the pre-fascist regime did not, or could not, save the country from 'anarchy' by legal means, fascism had to do it by force."[11]

The Political Elite

The fundamental idea that Gaetano Mosca (1858–1941) wanted to develop in his major work, *The Ruling Class*, was a new *political* theory of power. Like Pareto, he divided people in all societies into essentially two distinct classes: the ruling class (the political elite) and the class that is ruled (the masses). The ruling class always enjoys a monopoly of political power over the masses and directs society according to its own interests:

> In all societies . . . two classes of people appear—a class that rules and a class that is ruled. The first class, always the less numerous, performs all political functions, monopolizes power and enjoys the advantages that power brings, whereas the second, the more numerous class is directed and controlled by the first, in a manner that is now more or less legal, now more or less arbitrary and violent.[12]

This is not merely so with every known society of the past and the present; *all* societies *must* be so divided. Herein lies Mosca's argument for the "universal necessity" and "inevitability" of elite rule:

> Absolute equality has never existed in human societies: Political power never has been, and never will be, founded upon the explicit consent of majorities. It always has been, and it always will be, exercised by organized minorities, which have had, and will have, the means, varying as the times vary, to impose their supremacy on the multitudes.[13]

Mosca attempts here to establish "the real superiority of the concept of the ruling, or political, class," to show that "the varying structure of ruling classes has a preponderant importance in determining the political type, and also the level of civilization, of the different peoples."[14] Hence for Mosca it is the political apparatus of a given society and an organized minority (i.e., the political elite) that controls this apparatus—not the class structure—that determines the nature and movement of society and societal change.[15]

At one point, Mosca writes that "the discontent of the masses might succeed in deposing a ruling class," but, he immediately adds, "inevitably . . . there would have to be another organized minority within the masses themselves to discharge the functions of a ruling class."[16] As Mosca viewed the specific "functions" of ruling classes in universal terms, he could not envision a state and a society at the service of the laboring masses, as against a ruling class or an "organized minority within the masses."

Mosca's tautological arguments on the "inevitability" of elite rule as expressed above cast a heavy shadow on his work and call into question the accuracy of his observations. The "realistic science" that Mosca wanted to develop, writes Tom Bottomore, was in fact primarily intended to refute Marx's theory of class on two essential points:

> First, to show that the Marxist conception of a "ruling *class*" is erroneous, by demonstrating the continual circulation of elites, which prevents in most societies, and especially in modern industrial societies, the formation of a stable and closed ruling class; and secondly, to show that a classless society is impossible, since in every society there is, and must be, a minority which actually rules.[17]

"In the world in which we are living," Mosca wrote quite bluntly, "socialism will be arrested only if a realistic political science succeeds in demolishing the metaphysical and optimistic methods that prevail at present in social studies."[18] Targeting in particular Marx and his theory of historical materialism, Mosca argued that his book *The Ruling Class* "is a refutation of it."[19]

Although Mosca believed that the ruling classes throughout history "owe their special qualities not so much to the blood in their veins as to their very particular upbringing,"[20] and recognized that "social position, family tradition, the habits of the class in which we live, contribute more than is commonly supposed to the greater or lesser development of the qualities mentioned,"[21] he nonetheless failed to address the social implications of his own position by rejecting the class-struggle analysis of Marx and opting instead for a psychological theory of power based on an individualistic conception of human nature.

Bureaucratic Organization

Robert Michels (1876–1936), the third influential classical elite theorist, stressed that the source of the problem of elite rule lies in the nature and structure of bureaucratic organization.[22] He argued that the bureaucratic organization itself, irrespective of the intentions of bureaucrats, results in the formation of an elite-dominated society. Thus, regardless of ideological ends, organizational means would inevitably lead to oligarchic rule: "It is organization which gives birth to the domination of the elected over the electors, of the mandataries over the mandators, of the delegates over the delegators. Who says organization, says oligarchy."[23]

At the heart of Michels's theoretical model lie the three basic principles of elite formation that take place within the bureaucratic structure of political organization: (1) the need for specialized staff, facilities, and, above all, leaders; (2) the utilization of such specialized facilities by leaders within these organizations; and (3) the psychological attributes of the leaders (i.e., charisma).

Michels argued that the bureaucratic structure of modern political parties or organizations gives rise to specific conditions that corrupt the leaders and bureaucrats in such parties. These leaders, in turn, consolidate the power of the party leadership and set themselves apart from the masses. This is so, goes the argument, not only with the so-called democratic organizations of bourgeois society, but with socialist parties as well. Michels, a one-time "socialist," thought that if socialist parties, dedicated as they were to the highest egalitarian values, were undemocratic and elitist, then all organizations had to be elitist.

"Even the purest of idealists who attains to power for a few years," he wrote, "is unable to escape the corruption which the exercise of power carries in its train."[24] For Michels, this pointed to the conservative basis of (any) organization, since the *organizational form* as such was the basis of the conservatism, and this conservatism was the inevitable outcome of power attained through political organization. Hence, "political organization leads to power, but power is always conservative."[25]

Based on this reasoning, one might think that Michels was an anarchist; he was not. He insisted that *any* organization, *including those of the anarchists*, was subject to the "iron law":

> Anarchism, a movement on behalf of liberty, founded on the inalienable right of the human being over his own person, succumbs, no less than the Socialist Party, to the law of authoritarianism as soon as it abandons the region of pure thought and as soon as its adherents unite to form associations aiming at any sort of political activity.[26]

This same phenomenon of elitism/authoritarianism, argued Michels, also occurs at the individual level. Hence, to close the various gaps in his theory, Michels resorted to human-nature-based tautological arguments: Once a person ascends to the leadership level, he becomes a part of his new social milieu to the extent that he would resist ever leaving that position. The argument here is that the leader consolidates his power around the newly acquired condition and uses that power to serve *his* interests by perpetuating the maintenance of that power. In order to avoid this and eliminate authoritarianism, which comes about in "associations aiming at any sort of political activity," one must not "abandon the region of pure thought"! Herein lay the self-serving conservatism of Michels, who in the latter part of his life turned, like Pareto before him, to the cause of Italian fascism.

In his "Introduction" to a recent edition of Michels's book *Political Parties*, Seymour Martin Lipset writes:

> Michels, who had been barred from academic appointment in Germany for many years, ... left his position at the University of Basle to accept a chair at the University of Perugia offered to him personally by Benito Mussolini in 1928.[27]

Lipset goes on to point out: "Michels found his charismatic leader in Benito Mussolini. For him, Il Duce translated 'in a naked and brilliant form the aims of the multitude.'"[28] Finally, Michels "died as a supporter of fascist rule in Italy."[29]

Conclusion

The three major proponents of elite theory—Pareto, Mosca, and Michels—have provided a political theory of elites that they believed explains the nature and dynamics of power in modern society. Best exemplified in Mosca's characterization of the ruling class as the governing elite of full-time politicians in charge of the state apparatus and society in general, classical elite theory has argued in favor of a theory based on a conceptualization centered in bureaucratic organization, particularly in the sphere of politics. Hence, in a manner different from Weber's characterization of bureaucracy, which he viewed as a tool *of* power lodged in the economic (market) sphere, classical elite theorists—especially Mosca and Michels— argue that power in society resides in government and the governing elite.

Given its contempt for the masses and its acceptance of elite rule over them as an inevitable outcome of bureaucratic organization prevalent in modern politics, classical elite theory lends itself to antipopular, reactionary conclusions that have important political implications that are quite different from Weber's formulation of the question and are diametrically opposite to that of Marx and Engels regarding the prospects for change and social transformation in society today.

Notes

[1] Vilfredo Pareto, *The Mind and Society*, 4 vols., ed. Arthur Livingstone (New York: Harcourt, Brace, 1935).

[2] Ibid., 3:1423.

[3] Ibid., 1423–24; italics in the original.

[4] Ibid., 1430–31.

[5] Ibid., 1431.

[6] Ibid.

[7] Ibid., 1:40.

[8] Ibid., 3:1430.

⁹ Ibid.

¹⁰ Irving M. Zeitlin, *Ideology and the Development of Sociological Theory* (Englewood Cliffs, N.J.: Prentice Hall, 1968), 194.

¹¹ Ibid.

¹² Gaetano Mosca, *The Ruling Class* (New York: McGraw-Hill, 1939), 50.

¹³ Ibid., 326.

¹⁴ Ibid., 51.

¹⁵ Ibid., 329.

¹⁶ Ibid., 329.

¹⁷ Tom Bottomore, *Elites and Society* (Baltimore, Md.: Penguin, 1966), 17–18.

¹⁸ Mosca, *The Ruling Class*, 327.

¹⁹ Ibid., 447.

²⁰ Ibid., 62.

²¹ Ibid., 63.

²² Robert Michels, *Political Parties* (New York: Free Press, 1968).

²³ Ibid., 365.

²⁴ Ibid., 355.

²⁵ Ibid., 333.

²⁶ Ibid., 327–28.

²⁷ Seymour Martin Lipset, "Introduction," in Michels, *Political Parties*, 33.

²⁸ Ibid., 32.

²⁹ Ibid., 38.

Chapter	**5**	**FREUD ON THE DEVELOPMENT OF SOCIETY AND CIVILIZATION**

The controversies surrounding the development of a psychoanalytic theory of society earlier in this century have given rise to a number of critical approaches to Freudian psychology.[1] Some controversial figures, such as Wilhelm Reich, have attempted to develop a Marx–Freud synthesis to explore the political sources of mass psychology and explain the rise of fascism in Germany.[2] Others, such as Erich Fromm and Herbert Marcuse, have developed their own distinct versions of this synthesis, focusing on the cultural, ideological, and philosophical dimensions of Freudian theory that informs a critical analysis of modern society.[3]

This chapter examines Sigmund Freud's concept of human nature, the origins and development of society and civilization, and the nature of religion, so that we can better evaluate the significance of such syntheses and the extent and depth of Freud's contribution to classical social theory.

Human Nature and Character Structure

Sigmund Freud (1856–1939) viewed the individual as an organism driven by an instinctual energy called *libido*. Contrary to the arguments of some who have set forth a narrow, vulgar interpretation of libido as purely a sexual drive, others have maintained that the Freudian libidinal instinct

> is manifested not only in childhood sexuality, attachment to parents and brotherly love, but in art, work, aggression and just about all forms of human behavior involving emotional commitment including the feelings associated with the concepts "self-respect," "human dignity," "fraternity" and "equality."[4]

50

Moreover, Freud's broader characterization of libido as a more generalized drive for human satisfaction can be deduced from his observation suggesting that creative work may provide a primary release for libidinal energies:

> The possibility [work] offers of displacing a large amount of libidinal components, whether narcissistic, aggressive or even erotic, on to professional work and on to the human relations connected with it lends it a value by no means second to what it enjoys as something indispensible to the preservation and justification of existence in society. Professional activity is a source of special satisfaction if it is a freely chosen one—if, that is to say, by means of sublimation, it makes possible the use of existing inclinations, of persisting or constitutionally reinforced instinctual impulses.[5]

Focusing on the inner workings of human behavior, Freud concludes that there exists two contradictory processes: "After long doubts and vacillations," he writes, "we have decided to assume the existence of only two basic instincts, *Eros* and the destructive instinct."[6]

> The aim of the first of these basic instincts is to establish ever greater unities and to preserve them thus—in short, to bind together; the aim of the second, on the contrary, is to undo connections and so to destroy things. We may suppose that the final aim of the destructive instinct is to reduce living things to an inorganic state. For this reason we also call it the *death instinct*. . . .
> In biological functions the two basic instincts work against each other or combine with each other.[7]

These basic instincts, Freud tells us, represent "forces which we assume to exist behind the tensions caused by the needs of the id."[8] Furthermore, "they represent the somatic demands upon mental life. . . . [T]hey are the ultimate cause of all activity."[9]

These instincts, then, lie at the very core of human personality or character structure, and it is through the dynamic parts or mechanisms of this structure that one relates to others and to the external world. The three component parts of the individual's character structure, in the Freudian model, are the "id," the "ego," and the "super-ego"; together, they form the topography of the mind.

"The power of the id," Freud asserts, "expresses the true purpose of the individual organism's life. This consists in the satisfaction of its innate needs."[10]

> In the id there are no conflicts; contradictions and antitheses exist side by side, and often equalize matters between themselves by compromise formations. . . . [E]verything which goes on in the id is unconscious and remains so.[11]

Consequently,

> the core of our being, then, is formed by the obscure id, which has no direct relations with the external world and is accessible even to our own knowledge only through the medium of another agency of the mind. . . .
> The id, which is cut off from the external world, has its own world perception.[12]

In short, according to Freud, the id is our instinctual nature; it represents the drive for the satisfaction of our innate needs.

The ego, in contrast, is the organized part of the id. It mediates the demands of the id, on the one hand, and that of the realities of the external world as well as the super-ego, on the other. In Freud's words:

> the ego is in control of voluntary movement. It has the task of self-preservation. As regards *external* events, it performs that task by becoming aware of the stimuli from without. . . . As regards *internal* events, in relation to the id, it performs that task by gaining control over the demands of the instincts, by deciding whether they shall be allowed to obtain satisfaction, by postponing that satisfaction to times and circumstances favorable in the external world or by suppressing their excitations completely.[13]

Finally, the super-ego, according to Freud, is the conscience of internalized prohibitions of our culture. To the extent that these prohibitions imposed on individuals by society or civilization come to repress and frustrate libidinal energies, aggression is the result. If such aggression is not channeled through some social mechanism to release it, then the individual can become neurotic. Otherwise, the collective yearning to release repressed libidinal energies may trigger a social response that might have revolutionary political implications!

The Origins and Development of Society and Civilization

Society and civilization, in Freudian theory, have their roots in the material conditions of human social existence. Hence, for Freud, the rise and development of human societies must be explained through a concrete analysis of the social world. "Human civilization," Freud explains,

> includes on the one hand all the knowledge and capacity that men have acquired in order to control the forces of nature and extract its wealth for the satisfaction of human needs, and, on the other hand, all the regulations necessary in order to adjust the relations of men to one another and especially the distribution of the available wealth. The two trends of civilization are not independent of each other.[14]

The development of civilization, Freud argues, is thus the result of the physiological imperatives of survival (i.e., food, shelter, and physical security) and the society's need to organize social relations to maintain social order. "If we go back far enough," Freud writes, "we find that the first acts of civilization were the use of tools, the gaining of control over fire and the construction of dwellings."[15] At a certain point in history, humans realized that it would be to their advantage to work in cooperation with others to overcome the immense difficulties posed by nature, which threatened human survival. This cooperative work among individuals led to the formation of groups that were mutually beneficial for all. In Freud's words:

> After primal man had discovered that it lay in his own hands, literally, to improve his lot on earth by working, it cannot have been a matter of indifference to him whether another man worked with or against him. The other man acquired the value for him of a fellow-worker, with whom it was useful to live together. Even earlier, in his ape-like prehistory, man had adopted the habit of forming families, and the members of his family were probably his first helpers.[16]

For Freud, then, civilization is rooted in an individual's relationship with nature and with other individuals—in developing the necessary technology to sustain life and in satisfying his or her social needs. Thus, Freud gives us a materialist analysis of the rise and development of society and civilization. He argues that the human group has its roots in the material conditions of its social existence in nature and that the mechanism that facilitates this process is the family.

The family, through the social relationships it engages in, channels instinctual energies and forms the child's character structure. Through this process the family thus becomes the mechanism that produces and socializes children who are fitted to the social roles that society requires them to fulfill. In this way the family comes to play a key role in rationalizing and reinforcing the existing social order.[17]

The role of the family in facilitating the preservation of the modern social order is a central one in the Freudian view, as the social and class structure of society is transmitted to future generations through the socialization process that develops and matures in the family. Thus, "the social relationships of the family . . . channels instinctual energies and forms the child's character structure."[18] And with the development of this character structure, the family passes on to future generations the socially accepted roles that one's offspring acquire.

The recognition by some Marxist theorists of the process surrounding the role of the family in facilitating the maintenance of the status quo led to the development of the Marx-Freud synthesis in the earlier part of this century. The proponents of this approach developed their analysis to examine the reasons for the prevalance of false consciousness among the working class and see how it can be transformed into class consciousness that the working class family could promote to advance its class interests.

A recent proponent of this approach, Albert Szymanski, points out that, in his analysis of the family, Freud

> mistakenly assumes the logic of the family triad to be universal among "civilized" homo sapiens. The early synthesizers of Marx and Freud, on the other hand, put the family in historical context, recognizing Freud's universal family for the bourgeois family it is. They understood that families in different societies and different classes would have different logics and consequently would produce different typical character structures.[19]

To maintain their control over society, the dominant classes, through the institutions they control—which in turn have great influence on the family—channel behavior to conform to the values promoted by the existing social order. Thus, the development of a character structure that conforms to the prevailing status quo

> results in passive and dependent people who have internalized the necessities of class society and the capital accumulation process. Political conservatism among the masses of the oppressed thus becomes firmly rooted. False-consciousness among people who should be among the most active supporters of revolution is securely anchored by these mechanisms in the very psychology of the oppressed.[20]

Moreover:

> Conservatism and reaction in all its forms—religion, nationalism, fascism, etc.,—on the one hand ward off rational impulses [to freedom, dignity and self-determination] and on the other offer substitute gratifications in aggressive behavior towards other "races" and nations or against the very groups and individuals which advocate liberation. Racism, fascism and extreme nationalism

are thus firmly rooted in the character structures of large segments of the oppressed. These phenomena are consequently far more than mere attitudes, values, norms, or prejudices; they are based in the organization of our psychic energies.[21]

Thus, in order to eliminate these phenomena, which block the development of class consciousness, one "must remove the source of the energy behind such behavior, not just 're-educate,' i.e., the libidinal repression necessitated by the logic of capitalism must be eliminated by destroying that logic itself."[22]

Religion

Religion and religious ideas, for Freud, are likewise the manifestations of material conditions in social life; they reflect the basic social organization of society. Hence religious phenomena, Freud argues, must be explained from the standpoint of a materialist understanding of social reality—one that locates religion within the confines of existing society.

Perhaps one of the clearest statements of Freud's social conception of religion can be found in the following passage:

> Religion . . . is an attempt to get control over the sensory world, in which we are placed, by means of the wish world which we have developed inside us as a result of biological and psychological necessities. But it cannot achieve its end. Its doctrines carry with them the stamp of the times in which they originate, the ignorant childhood days of the human race.[23]

Arguing that religion plays an illusory role and mystifies the nature of human relations in society, Freud proclaims the abolition of religion as the first step toward the demystification of social reality, hence clearing the way for the realization of true human potential. In his dialogue with his imaginary opponent in *The Future of an Illusion*, Freud argues that "religious doctrines . . . should cease to be put forward as the reasons for the precepts of civilization."[24] Moreover, "those historical residues," he adds, have helped us to view religious teachings, as it were, as neurotic relics, and we may now argue that the time has probably come, as it does in an analytic treatment, for replacing the effects of repression by the results of the rational operation of the intellect. We may foresee, but hardly regret, that such a process of remolding will not stop at renouncing the solemn transfiguration of cultural percepts, but that a general revision of them will result in many of them being done away with.[25]

"[R]eligious doctrines will have to be discarded," Freud insists,

no matter whether the first attempts fail, or whether the first substitutes prove to be untenable. . . . [I]n the long run nothing can withstand reason and experience, and the contradiction which religion offers to both is all too palpable.[26]

Through the abolition of religion, then, humanity will be able to free itself from illusions and actively intervene in history to liberate itself from repression and move toward the satisfaction of truly human needs—needs that precisely form the very core of the human experience.

Conclusion

The above analysis of the Freudian approach in classical social theory reveals a number of strands in the application of psychoanalytic theory to explain social reality. We have argued that once they are stripped of their biological connotations, Freud's arguments in essence are socially based and represent the inner workings of social life that he was able to express through his materialist analysis of society and the social order within which the individual is situated. Thus, for Freud, the discontented individual becomes stressed because society limits individual freedoms by repressing his or her innate psychological drives. Further, the major institutions of society—such as the family, the state, and religion—play a pivotal role in perpetuating this condition to maintain social order. From a dialectical standpoint, however, these very same institutions can also become key instruments of change that help *transform* society and achieve genuine freedom for the individual and the social collectivity as a whole.

The significance of the Freudian model, then, is such that, if interpreted within its social and material context, it can add an important dimension to sociological analysis and make a significant contribution to the body of knowledge that represents the best in classical social theory.

Notes

[1] For a critical analysis of the origins and development of psychoanalysis in the United States, see Harry K. Wells, *The Failure of Psychoanalysis* (New York: International Publishers, 1963); and C.P. Oberndorf, *A History of Psychoanalysis in America* (New York: Grune, 1953). See also Martin Jay, *The Dialectical Imagination* (Boston: Little Brown, 1973), chap. 3.

[2] See, for example, Wilhelm Reich, *Character Analysis* (New York: Orgone Institute Press, 1949); idem, *The Mass Psychology of Fascism* (New York: Farrar, Strauss and Giroux, 1970); and idem, *Sex Pol; Essays, 1929–1934* (New York: Random House, 1972).

[3] For a sampling of Fromm's writings, see Erich Fromm, *Beyond the Chains of Illusion* (New York: Simon and Schuster, 1962); and idem, *The Crisis of Psychoanalysis* (New York: Holt, Rinehart, Winston, 1970). For some of Marcuse's most influential works, see Herbert Marcuse, *One Dimensional Man* (Boston: Beacon Press, 1964); and idem, *Eros and Civilization* (New York: Vintage Books, 1968).

[4] Al Szymanski, "The Revolutionary Uses of Freudian Theory," *Social Praxis* 5, nos. 1–2 (1976): 46.

[5] Sigmund Freud, *Civilization and Its Discontents* (New York: Norton, 1962), 27.

[6] Sigmund Freud, *An Outline of Psychoanalysis* (New York: Norton, 1949), 20.

[7] Ibid., 20–21.

[8] Ibid., 19.

[9] Ibid.

[10] Ibid.

[11] Sigmund Freud, *The Question of Lay Analysis* (New York: Norton, 1950), 36, 38.

[12] Freud, *An Outline of Psychoanalysis*, 108–9.

[13] Ibid., 15–16.

[14] Sigmund Freud, *The Future of an Illusion* (Garden City, NY: Anchor, 1961), 2–3.

[15] Freud, *Civilization and Its Discontents*, 37.

[16] Ibid., 46.

[17] Szymanski, "The Revolutionary Uses of Freudian Theory," 32.

[18] Ibid., 30.
[19] Ibid.
[20] Ibid., 36.
[21] Ibid.
[22] Ibid.
[23] Sigmund Freud, *New Introductory Lectures on Psychoanalysis*, 168.
[24] Freud, *The Future of an Illusion*, 72.
[25] Ibid., 72–73.
[26] Ibid., 88–89.

Chapter	**6**	GRAMSCI AND LENIN ON IDEOLOGY, THE STATE, AND REVOLUTION

While the classical elite theorists held the masses in contempt and sided with the ruling classes as the engines of social development, V.I. Lenin (1870–1924) and Antonio Gramsci (1891–1937), like Marx and Engels before them, threw in their lot with the laboring masses and saw the working class as the leading revolutionary force to transform capitalist society.

This chapter takes a brief look at the central arguments of Gramsci and Lenin on the nature and role of the state and ideological hegemony and explores the underlying class contradictions of capitalist society which, they argued, would lead to its revolutionary transformation.

Class Struggle and the State

Outlined in its clearest and most concise form in his classic work *The State and Revolution*, Lenin explains that in all class societies, the *class essence* of the state's rule over society is rooted in domination and exploitation by a propertied ruling class of the propertyless oppressed class.

In our epoch, writes Lenin, "every state in which private ownership of the land and means of production exists, in which capital dominates, however democratic it may be, is a capitalist state, a machine used by the capitalists to keep the working class and the poor peasants in subjection."[1]

Democracy in capitalist society, Lenin points out, is always bound by "the narrow limits set by capitalist exploitation, and consequently always remains, in effect, a democracy for the minority, only for the propertied classes, only for the rich."[2]

> Freedom in capitalist society always remains about the
> same as it was in the ancient Greek republics: freedom
> for the slave-owners. Owing to the conditions of capi-
> talist exploitation, the modern wage slaves are so crushed
> by want and poverty that "they cannot be bothered with
> democracy," "cannot be bothered with politics"; in the
> ordinary, peaceful course of events, the majority of the
> population is debarred from participation in public and
> political life. . . .
>
> Democracy for an insignificant minority, demo-
> cracy for the rich—that is the democracy of capitalist
> society. . . .
>
> Marx grasped this *essence* of capitalist democracy
> splendidly when, in analyzing the experience of the
> Commune, he said that the oppressed are allowed once
> every few years to decide which particular representa-
> tives of the oppressing class shall represent and repress
> them in parliament![3]

"People always have been the foolish victims of deception and
self-deception in politics," Lenin continues elsewhere, "and they
always will be until they have learnt to seek out the *interests* of some
class or other behind all moral, religious, political and social
phrases, declarations and promises."[4]

In class society, Lenin points out, the state has always been "an
organ or instrument of violence exercised by one class against
another."[5] And in capitalist society, this violence is exercised by the
capitalist class against the working class. In an important passage in
The State and Revolution, Lenin stresses that the state in capitalist
society is not only the political organ of the capitalist class; it is
structured in such a way that it guarantees the class rule of the
capitalists and, short of a revolutionary rupture, its entrenched
power is practically unshakable:

> A democratic republic is the best possible political shell
> for capitalism, and, therefore, once capital has gained
> possession of this very best shell . . . it establishes its
> power so securely, so firmly, that *no* change of persons,
> institutions or parties in the bourgeois-democratic re-
> public can shake it.[6]

The question remains: With the obvious contradictions and conflicts between labor and capital, and with the ever-more visible unity of capital and the state, how is capital able to convince broad segments of the laboring masses of the legitimacy of its class rule and the rule of the capitalist state over society?

Ideological Hegemony

In explaining the process by which the capitalist class disseminates its ideology through control of the state and its dominance over society, Antonio Gramsci drew attention to the ideological apparatuses of the capitalist state and introduced the concept of bourgeois cultural and ideological *hegemony*.[7] He stressed that it is not enough for the capitalist class simply to take control of the state machine and rule society directly through force and coercion; it must also convince the oppressed classes of the legitimacy of its rule: "The state is the entire complex of practical and theoretical activities with which the ruling class not only justifies and maintains its dominance, but manages to win the active consent of those over whom it rules."[8] Through its dominance of the superstructural organs of the state, the ruling class controls and shapes the ideas, hence consciousness, of the masses. Thus:

> Hegemony involves the successful attempts of the dominant class to use its political, moral, and intellectual leadership to establish its view of the world as all-inclusive and universal, and to shape the interests and needs of subordinate groups.[9]

With the acceptance of its ideas and the legitimization of its rule, the capitalist class is able to exercise control and domination of society through its ideological hegemony at the level of the superstructure with the aid and instrumentality of the state. Gramsci, writes Martin Carnoy, "assigned to the State part of this function of promoting a single (bourgeois) concept of reality, and, therefore, gave the State a more extensive (enlarged) role in perpetuating class,"[10] hence preventing the development of working-class consciousness. As such, it was not merely lack of understanding of their position in the economic process that kept workers from comprehending their class role, nor was it only the "private" institutions of society, such as religion, that were responsible for keeping the working class from self-realization, but it was the *State itself* that was involved in reproducing the relations of production. In other words, the State was much more than the coercive apparatus of the bourgeoisie; the State included the hegemony of the bourgeoisie in the superstructure.[11]

Although the dialectics of the accumulation process, which involves first and foremost the exploitation of labor, ultimately results in class struggle, civil war, and revolution to seize state power, the *ideological hegemony* of the ruling class, operating through the state itself, prolongs bourgeois class rule and institutionalizes and legitimizes exploitation. Gramsci argued that "the system's real strength does not lie in the violence of the ruling class or the coercive power of its state apparatus, but in the acceptance by the ruled of a 'conception of the world' which belongs to the rulers."[12] "False consciousness"—or lack of working-class consciousness and adoption of bourgeois ideas by the laboring masses—Gramsci argued, was the result of a complex process of bourgeois ideological hegemony that, operating through the superstructural (i.e., cultural, ideological, religious, and political) institutions of capitalist society, above all the bourgeois state, came to obtain the consent of the masses in convincing them of the correctness and superiority of the bourgeois worldview.

In his doctrine of "hegemony," Gramsci saw that the dominant class did not have to rely solely on the coercive power of the State or even its direct economic power to rule; rather, through its hegemony, expressed in the civil society *and* the State, the ruled could be persuaded to accept the system of beliefs of the ruling class and to share its social, cultural, and moral values.[13]

"The philosophy of the ruling class," writes Giuseppe Fiori, "passes through a whole tissue of complex vulgarizations to emerge as 'common sense': that is, the philosophy of the masses, who accept the morality, the customs, the institutionalized behavior of the society they live in."[14] "The problem for Gramsci then," Fiori continues, "is to understand *how* the ruling class has managed to win the consent of the subordinate classes in this way; and then, to see how the latter will manage to overthrow the old order and bring about a new one of universal freedom."[15]

The increasing awareness of the working class of this process, hence the development of working-class consciousness, stresses Gramsci, helps expand the emerging class struggle from the economic and social spheres into the sphere of politics and ideology, so the struggle against capitalist ideology promoted by the bourgeois state and other ruling-class institutions becomes just as important, perhaps more so, as the struggle against capital develops and matures in other spheres of society. Countering the ideological hegemony of the capitalist class through the active participation of workers in their own collective organizations, the class-conscious organs of work- ers' power—militant trade unions, workers' political parties, and so forth—come to play a decisive role in gaining the political support of the laboring masses. In turn, through their newly gained aware- ness of their own class interests, the workers transcend the bounds of bourgeois ideological hegemony and develop their own counter (proletarian) political outlook—a process that accelerates with the further development of proletarian class consciousness. Thus, as the struggle against the state becomes an important part of the class struggle in general, the struggle against capitalism takes on a truly *political* and *ideological* content.

Gramsci's contribution to the Marxist theory of the state and of bourgeois ideological hegemony, then, both affirms *and* extends the analyses of the Marxist classics and advances our understanding of the processes of ruling-class domination and hegemony and the responses needed for the transformation of capitalist society.

The State and Revolution

Writing in August 1917, on the eve of the Great October Socialist Revolution in Russia, Lenin pointed out both the class nature of the state *and*, more important, the necessity of its revolutionary over- throw:

> If the state is the product of the irreconcilability of class
> antagonisms, if it is a power standing *above* society and
> *"alienating* itself *more and more* from it," it is clear that
> the liberation of the oppressed class is impossible not
> only without a violent revolution, *but also without the
> destruction* of the apparatus of state power which was
> created by the ruling class and which is the embodiment
> of this "alienation."[16]

Thus, for Lenin the transformation of capitalist society involves a revolutionary process in which a class-conscious working class, led by a disciplined workers' party, comes to adopt a radical solution to its continued exploitation and oppression under the yoke of capital and exerts its organized political force in a revolutionary rupture to take state power.

The victory of the working class in this struggle for power and control over society leads to the establishment of a socialist workers' state. The socialist state constitutes a new kind of state ruled by the working class and the laboring masses. The cornerstone of a workers' state, emerging out of capitalism, is the abolition of private property in the major means of production and an end to the exploitation of labor for private profit.

The establishment of a revolutionary dictatorship of the prole-tariat (as against the dictatorship of capital) is what distinguishes the socialist state from its capitalist counterpart. As the class essence of the state lies at the heart of an analysis of the nature and role of the state in different epochs throughout history, the class nature of the socialist state gives us clues to the nature and role of the state in a socialist society developing toward communism. For, as Marx has pointed out in *Critique of the Gotha Program*, the dictatorship of the proletariat (i.e., the class rule of the working class) is a transitional phase between capitalism and communism:

> Between capitalist and communist society lies the pe-
> riod of the revolutionary transformation of the one into
> the other. Corresponding to this is also a political
> transition period in which the state can be nothing but
> *the revolutionary dictatorship of the proletariat.*[17]

During this period, the state represents and defends the interests of the working class against capital and all other vestiges of reactionary exploitative classes, which, overthrown and dislodged from power, attempt in a multitude of ways to recapture the state through a counterrevolution.

"The theory of the class struggle, applied by Marx to the question of the state and the socialist revolution," writes Lenin,

> leads as a matter of course to the recognition of the *political rule* of the proletariat, of its dictatorship, i.e., of undivided power directly backed by the armed force of the people. The overthrow of the bourgeoisie can be achieved only by the proletariat becoming the *ruling class*, capable of crushing the inevitable and desperate resistance of the bourgeoisie, and of organizing *all* the working and exploited people for the new economic system.[18]

In this context, then, the proletarian state has a dual role to play: (1) to break the resistance of its class enemies (the exploiting classes); and (2) to protect the revolution and begin the process of socialist construction.

The Withering Away of the State

The class character of the new state under the dictatorship of the proletariat takes on a new form and content, according to Lenin: "During this period the state must inevitably be a state that is democratic *in a new way* (for the proletariat and the propertyless in general) and dictatorial *in a new way* (against the bourgeoisie)."[19] Thus,

> *simultaneously* with an immense expansion of democracy, which *for the first time* becomes democracy for the poor, democracy for the people, and not democracy for the money-bags, the dictatorship of the proletariat imposes a series of restrictions on the freedom of the oppressors, the exploiters, the capitalists.[20]

Used primarily to suppress these forces and build the material base of a classless, egalitarian society, the socialist state begins to wither away once there is no longer any need for it. As Engels points out:

> The first act in which the state really comes forward as the representative of society as a whole—the taking possession of the means of production in the name of society—is at the same time its last independent act as a state. The interference of the state power in social relations becomes superfluous in one sphere after another, and then ceases of itself. The government of persons is replaced by the administration of things and the direction of the processes of production. The state is not "abolished," *it withers away.*[21]

In this sense, the state no longer exists in the fully matured communist stage, for there is no longer the need in a classless society for an institution that is, by definition, an instrument of class rule through force and violence. Lenin writes:

> Only in communist society, when the resistance of the capitalists has been completely crushed, when the capitalists have disappeared, when there are no classes (i.e., when there is no distinctions between the members of society as regards their relation to the social means of production), *only* then "the state . . . ceases to exist," and "*it becomes possible to speak of freedom.*" Only then will a truly complete democracy become possible and be realized, a democracy without any exceptions whatever.[22]

It is in this broader, transitional context that the class nature and tasks of the state in socialist society must be understood and evaluated, according to Lenin.

Thus, Lenin characterized the period of transition to communist society as exhibiting an infinitely higher form of democracy than that found in capitalist society, for democracy under socialism, he argued, is democracy for the masses, democracy for the great majority of the laboring population working together to build an egalitarian, classless society.

Notes

[1] V.I. Lenin, *The State*, in Karl Marx, Frederick Engels, and V.I. Lenin, *On Historical Materialism* (New York: International Publishers, 1974), 641.

[2] V.I. Lenin, *The State and Revolution*, in V.I. Lenin, *Selected Works in Three Volumes* (Moscow: Progress Publishers, 1975), 2:301.

[3] Ibid., 301–2.

[4] V.I. Lenin, "The Three Sources and Three Component Parts of Marxism," in V.I. Lenin, *Selected Works in One Volume* (New York: International Publishers, 1971), 24.

[5] Lenin, *The State and Revolution*, 374.

[6] Ibid., 247.

[7] By *hegemony*, Gramsci meant the ideological predominance of the dominant ruling class(es) over the subordinate. At the same time, and in response to this, he introduced the concept of counterhegemony, which occurs when the proletariat, with the aid of "organic" intellectuals, exerts hegemony and exercises its superiority over society through the establishment of a proletarian socialist state.

[8] Antonio Gramsci, *Prison Notebooks* (New York: International Publishers, 1971), 244.

[9] Martin Carnoy, *The State and Political Theory* (Princeton: Princeton University Press, 1984), 70.

[10] Ibid., 66.

[11] Ibid.; emphasis in the original.

[12] Giuseppe Fiori, *Antonio Gramsci, Life of a Revolutionary* (London: New Left Books, 1970), 238.

[13] Carnoy, *The State and Political Theory*, 87.

[14] Fiori, *Antonio Gramsci*, 238.

[15] Ibid.

[16] Lenin, *The State and Revolution*, 242; emphasis in the original.

[17] Karl Marx, *Critique of the Gotha Programme*, in Karl Marx and Frederick Engels, *Selected Works* (New York: International Publishers, 1972), 331; emphasis in the original. For an extended discussion on the concept of the "dictatorship of the proletariat," see Etienne Balibar, *On the Dictatorship of the Proletariat* (London: New Left Books, 1977).

[18] Lenin, *The State and Revolution*, 255; emphasis in the original.

[19] Ibid., 262; emphasis in the original.

[20] Ibid., 302; emphasis in the original.

[21] F. Engels, *Anti-Duhring* (New York: International Publishers, 1976), 307.

[22] Lenin, *The State and Revolution*, 302–3; emphasis in the original.

Chapter	7	KOLLONTAI ON CLASS, GENDER, AND PATRIARCHY

This chapter examines the contributions of Alexandra Kollontai (1872–1952) to the study of gender, patriarchy, and the position of women in capitalist society and provides an analysis of her views on "the women's question," as well as the processes engendering the social emancipation of women.[1]

Kollontai was one of the most outspoken proponents of women's rights at the beginning of this century. Keenly aware of the oppression of women in capitalist society and adamantly opposed to the patriarchal structures imposed on women that assured their subordination over the centuries, Kollontai took up the study of the women's question to advance the cause of women's rights and thereby contribute to women's total social emancipation. To this end, she undertook a serious study of the nature and dynamics of women's oppression in contemporary capitalist society and thus helped develop a theory and practice for the liberation of women.

Capitalism, Patriarchy, and the Women's Question

The principal idea in the approach taken by Kollontai to the women's question, which sharply differed from that adopted by her feminist contemporaries, was the recognition of existing social relations—above all, relations of production or class relations—as the determinant of various aspects of life in class society, including the subordination and oppression of women. "The conditions and forms of production," Kollontai wrote in *The Social Basis of the Women's Question*, "have subjugated women throughout human history, and have gradually relegated them to the position of oppression and dependence in which most of them existed until now."[2] Pointing out that "specific economic factors were behind the subordination of women"[3] throughout history, she went on to argue that:

69

A colossal upheaval of the entire social and economic structure was required before women could begin to retrieve the significance and independence they had lost. . . . The same forces which for thousands of years enslaved women now, at a further stage of development, are leading them along the path of freedom and independence.[4]

This is so because class society in general, and capitalism in particular, is producing and reproducing its class contradictions. By drawing in more and more women into the labor force and exploiting them at a level much higher than working men, Kollontai argued, capitalism is inevitably contributing to the future liberation of women as women begin to organize and struggle alongside men for the liberation of their class, working class—an observation similar to the one made earlier by Engels.

Kollontai's analysis of the nature and sources of women's oppression led her to look for a class solution to the emancipation of women. The rights of women, she argued, could not be achieved while society was organized on the basis of private profit. Going beyond the critique of capitalism and the exploitation of labor in general, Kollontai placed the interests of women workers at the forefront of her analysis and examined the struggles of working women and their families in the late-nineteenth-century capitalist society that preceded the bourgeois women's movement that emerged later during this period, bringing into sharp focus the class content of women's rights under capitalism.

Examining the origins of the bourgeois women's movement, Kollontai traced the development of a broader struggle for women's rights as it unfolded during the second half of the nineteenth century. Viewing the condition of women from a class perspective, Kollontai differentiated the interests of working-class women from those of bourgeois and petty bourgeois women and argued that well before the birth of the bourgeois women's movement, working class women had entered the world of labor and struggled for their rights as part of the struggles of the working class in general. This class-based approach to the women's question allowed her to reach different political conclusions than the bourgeois feminists of her time and laid bare the ideological split that defined the two leading positions in the early women's movement.

Class, Gender, and Feminism

Providing a class-analysis approach to the study of women's position in capitalist society, Kollontai, like Rosa Luxemburg and Clara Zetkin, defined the rights and interests of women on the basis of their *class* position, not their gender alone. She developed a sharp critique of the feminist movement for representing the interests of only a segment of the female population—bourgeois women. Siding with the working class politically and advocating the transformation of capitalist society and the building of socialism, Kollontai focused her attention on *working women* and saw their emancipation as part of the process of emancipation of the working class from capitalist exploitation.

Stating her position in sharp contrast to that of the feminists, Kollontai framed the women's question in strictly *class* terms. "The women's world," she wrote, "is divided, just as is the world of men, into two camps":

The interests and aspirations of one group of women bring it close to the bourgeois class, while the other group has close connections with the proletariat, and its claims for liberation encompass a full solution to the woman question.[5]

She went on to point out that, although both of these groups advocate the liberation of women from their historic oppression, their goals and interests are different because "each of the groups unconsciously takes its starting point from the interests of its own class."[6]

The class essence of women's rights, as manifested in the position of women in society with respect to labor, is clearly driven home in Kollontai's works when she focuses on the problems of working women as they experience them in their daily lives. The abstract, generalized pronouncements of feminist organizations, advocating women's rights in a broader context of female oppression in capitalist society, are thus given concrete meaning in Kollontai's works as she addresses the manifestations of production based on private profit. The exploitation of labor, especially female labor, takes on a special *class* meaning, differentiating the experiences and thereby the interests of women of different classes—a distinction that has important political implications as well. This is pointed out very clearly in much of Kollontai's writings that directly address the feminists.

"The feminists," she points out, "seek equality in the framework of the existing class society; in no way do they attack the basis of this society. They fight for prerogatives for themselves, without challenging the existing prerogatives and privileges."[7] Thus, "however apparently radical the demands of the feminists," she argues, "one must not lose sight of the fact that the feminists cannot, on account of their class position, fight for that fundamental transformation of the contemporary economic and social structure of society without which the liberation of women cannot be complete."[8]

The liberation of working women, and of women in general, cannot therefore be achieved without a major transformation of the existing capitalist social order, which requires, for Kollontai, a revolutionary restructuring of the social, economic, and political life that defined the cultural parameters of society in the early twentieth century.

Social Revolution and the Liberation of Women

The fundamental question for Kollontai regarding the liberation of women was the nature and source of change, which divided the women's movement along class lines. Should women's struggles primarily focus on the manifestations of existing exploitative relations in capitalist society, or should they confront head-on the very structures of capitalism that have generated these manifestations in the first place? Kollontai puts the question this way: "Can political equality in the context of the retention of the entire capitalist-exploiter system free the working woman from that abyss of evil and suffering which pursues and oppresses her both as a woman and as a human being?"[9] And she answers it as follows:

The more aware among proletarian women realize that neither political nor juridical equality can solve the women's question in all its aspects. While women are compelled to sell their labor power and bear the yoke of capitalism, while the present exploitative system of producing new values continues to exist, they cannot become free and independent persons.[10]

Thus, the aim of the women workers, Kollontai points out, "is to abolish all privileges deriving from birth or wealth" and that in this sense they are "fighting for the common class cause, while at the same time outlining and putting forward those needs and demands that most nearly affect themselves as women, housewives and mothers."[11] The struggles of working women, therefore, "are part and parcel of the common workers' cause!"[12]

There was a time when working men thought that they alone must bear on their shoulders the brunt of the struggle against capital, that they alone must deal with the "old world" without the help of their womenfolk. However, as working-class women entered the labor market by need, by the fact that husband or father is unemployed, working men became aware that to leave women behind in the ranks of the "non-class-conscious" was to damage their cause and hold it back. The greater the number of conscious fighters, the greater the chances of success. . . .

Every special, distinct form of work among the women of the working class is simply a means of arousing the consciousness of the woman worker and drawing her into the ranks of those fighting for a better future. . . . [The] meticulous work undertaken to arouse the self-consciousness of the woman worker are serving the cause . . . of the unification of the working class.[13]

It is in this context of the broader interests of the working class as a whole that Kollontai developed her understanding of the interplay between class, gender, and patriarchy and identified the centrality of the exploitation of labor for private profit as the basis of the oppression and exploitation of working women in capitalist society.

Notes

[1] For a brief biographical sketch of Kollontai, see the excellent compilation on numerous women social theorists by Mary Jo Deegan, ed., *Women in Sociology* (Westport, Conn.: Greenwood Press, 1991), 231–38. See also Sheila Rowbotham, *Women, Resistance, and Revolution* (New York: Penguin, 1972), 134–60.

[2] Alexandra Kollontai, "The Social Basis of the Woman Question," in *Selected Writings of Alexandra Kollontai*, ed. Alix Holt (Westport, Conn.: Lawrence Hill, 1978), 61.

[3] Ibid., 58.

[4] Ibid., 61.

[5] Ibid., 59.

[6] Ibid.

[7] Ibid.

[8] Ibid., 59–60.

[9] Kollontai, in I.M. Dazhina et al., eds., *Alexandra Kollontai: Selected Articles and Speeches* (New York: International Publishers, 1984), 33–34.

[10] Ibid., 34.

[11] Ibid., 64.

[12] Ibid.

[13] Ibid., 62–65.

8 DU BOIS AND FRAZIER ON RACE, CLASS, AND SOCIAL EMANCIPATION

This chapter examines the ideas of two of the most prominent black social theorists of the early twentieth century, William Edward Burghardt Du Bois (1868–1963) and Edward Franklin Frazier (1894–1962).[1] Together, Du Bois and Frazier set the standard for the study of race relations in the United States in the early decades of this century and made a major contribution to social theory on the relationship between race and class.

Race Relations and the Color Line

At the beginning of the twentieth century, in 1901, W.E.B. Du Bois proclaimed: "The problem of the twentieth century is the problem of the color line."[2] Subsequently, Frazier, following his mentor, undertook the study of race relations in America to expose the predicament of African Americans, documenting the nature and depth of their oppression. Despite their political differences, together Du Bois and Frazier made a major contribution to the sociology of race and race relations in America in the twentieth century.

W.E.B. Du Bois, writes Meyer Weinberg, "was one of the greatest intellectuals America ever produced. If the intellectual is a tensor between scholarship and social action, Du Bois fulfilled the role with the highest distinction."[3] In his "Foreword" to Manning Marable's biography of Du Bois, John Milton Cooper, Jr., writes:

W.E.B. Du Bois ranks, along with Frederick Douglass, Booker T. Washington, and Martin Luther King, Jr., as one of the four greatest black Americans in the nation's history. Like them, he was a leader of his people and a man who sought to share fully in their lot. . . . [M]ore than any other person, he uncovered and interpreted black Americans' African roots and theorized about their ties to the larger nonwhite world. Du Bois deserves the title of first and greatest Afro-American.[4]

"There is no outstanding Afro-American creative figure of the twentieth century," writes another distinguished historian and editor of Du Bois's numerous works, Herbert Aptheker, "who did not, at some point, draw inspiration and gather aid directly from their Dean."[5] Indeed, Du Bois was the most celebrated intellectual and social activist in the black community until his death in 1963.

E. Franklin Frazier was among those exposed to Du Bois's ideas while a graduate student at Howard University—ideas that shaped the content and direction of studies taken up by a new generation of black intellectuals in subsequent decades. "Frazier's work and self-identity," writes Anthony Platt, "were consistently driven by a sense of moral outrage at any kind of social inequality and a relentless, burning hatred of racism."[6]

Although his contributions were much more modest, Frazier was no less political than Du Bois. They made different kinds of contributions and operated in different arenas, but, like Du Bois, it was a rare day when Frazier did not think about the struggle against inequality.[7]

Concerned at the same time with the social makeup of the black community and its internal class dynamics, which were in the process of maturation, Frazier addressed the developing class distinctions that were increasingly determining the nature and dynamics of social relations among blacks in the mid twentieth century—trends that developed further in the latter part of the century.[8]

Placed in historical context, the ideas and works of Du Bois and Frazier provide us much insight into the social condition of African Americans over the past two hundred years and give us the tools of analysis to develop an interpretation of their predicament in American society.

From Slavery to Freedom:
The Predicament of African Americans

Under slavery and formal freedom, the African American experience is captured brilliantly in the works of W.E.B. Du Bois, whose great-grandfather was a slave. Born barely two years after the end of the Civil War, Du Bois became keenly aware of the experience of slavery in the social, economic, political, and psychological makeup of African Americans in the closing decades of the nineteenth century.

The slave system in the South set the parameters of life for millions of black slaves who were denied citizenship and basic human rights for more than a century.

> With the new world came fatally the African slave trade and Negro slavery in the Americas. There were new cruelties, new hatreds of human beings, and new degradations of human labor. The temptation to degrade human labor was made vaster and deeper by the incredible accumulation of wealth based on slave labor, by the boundless growth of greed, and by world-wide organization for new agricultural crops, new techniques in industry, and world-wide trade.[9]

The slaves, Du Bois explains, "could be bought and sold, could move from place to place only with permission, were forbidden to learn to read or write, legally could never hold property or marry."[10] This oppressive condition that the slaves experienced continued until the late nineteenth century.

> Then came the war, which was not started with the idea of liberating the slaves, but which soon showed the North that freedom for the Negro was not only a logical conclusion of the war, but the only possible physical conclusion. Two hundred thousand black men were drafted in the army and the whole slave support to the Confederacy was threatened with withdrawal. Insurrection was in the air and the emancipation of the slaves was needed to save the Union. . . .

The Negro was freed as a penniless, landless, naked, ignorant laborer. Very few Negroes owned property in the South; a larger number of the race in the South were field hands, servants of the lowest class.[11]

Over the years, the ex-slaves became transformed into farm laborers and then into industrial workers in the mines and mills of modern capital as wage labor. Thus, during the century following emancipation, more and more blacks became part of an expanding working class, and the black community in general began to undergo internal social differentiation such that a more complex class structure began to emerge among blacks as well. The intersection of race and class thus took on new meaning in the discussions and debates that began to surface among black intellectuals in addressing the problems of race and class in contemporary American society.

The Question of Race and Class

The changing dynamics of the developing class structure among blacks led Du Bois and Frazier to take up a closer examination of the relationship between race and class.

Du Bois had earlier (at the turn of the century) observed that "the problem of the twentieth century is the problem of the color line," and by the early 1920s had rejected the class analysis approach to the study of black people in America by asking: "How far, for instance, does the dogma of the 'class struggle' apply to black folk in the United States today?"[12] He answered it this way:

The colored group is not yet divided into capitalists and laborers. There are only the beginnings of such a division. In one hundred years, if we develop along conventional lines, we would have such fully separated classes.[13]

Although he continued to hold on to these views during the 1930s and 1940s, Du Bois was always aware of the potential development of classes and class conflict among blacks if current trends of capitalist expansion in America were to encroach on the black community in the future:

> The main danger and the central question of the capitalistic development through which the Negro-American group is forced to go is the question of the ultimate control of the capital which they must raise and use. If this capital is going to be controlled by a few men for their own benefit, then we are destined to suffer from our own capitalists exactly what we are suffering from white capitalists today.[14]

By midcentury, the dynamics of the changing class structure among blacks that was manifesting itself in the black community convinced Du Bois to supplement his earlier observations by stating:

> [During the 1930s] I repudiated the idea that Negroes were in danger of inner class division based on income and exploitation. Here again I was wrong. Twenty years later, by 1950, it was clear that the great machine of big business was sweeping not only the mass of white Americans . . . it had also and quite naturally swept Negroes into the same maelstrom.[15]

He went on to point out that, with the fall of official segregation in public accommodations and schools, blacks "will be divided into classes even more sharply than now."[16] By 1960, Manning Marable points out, "Du Bois argued that 'class divisions' within Negro communities had so divided blacks 'that they are no longer [one] single body. They are different sets of people with different sets of interests.'"[17]

Adopting more and more a class-analysis approach to the race question, Du Bois during the later years of his life (in the 1950s and early 1960s), as Gerald Horne points out, began to develop "firm and decided views about the basis for race discrimination" in class terms: "He continually pointed to the wage differential between black and white workers as the material basis for racism."[18] In this way, Horne observes, "Du Bois was edging away" from his earlier view that "the problem of the twentieth century is the problem of the color line" and "edging toward the view that the twentieth century's problem was labor."[19]

Frazier, like Du Bois, also went through a transformation in his ideas on the causes and consequences of racism. Going beyond his earlier, social-psychological studies of race relations and the black family, Frazier's views about racism later became more and more informed by social class.[20] "Influenced by the class-based theories of left intellectuals and organizations," writes Platt, "by the 1930s . . . his writings tended to reinterpret the history of race relations through a prism of exploitation."[21]

"The introduction of the Negro into America," Frazier pointed out, "was due to the economic expansion of Europe" and "the fate of Negro slavery was determined by economic forces"; in this sense, "the Negro's status in the United States," he stressed, "has been bound up, in the final analysis, with the role which the Negro has played in the economic system."[22] Framing the problem in such broader, historical and structural terms, Frazier, as Platt points out, "located the fundamental roots of racism in the dynamics of class relations on a global scale."[23]

Racism, Class Conflict, and Social Emancipation

Both Du Bois and Frazier understood the dynamics of racism as a manifestation of class conflict. They understood, therefore, that social emancipation would be the outcome of a resolution of the struggle between the chief opposing classes in society. Although Du Bois's views on the forms the struggle would take differed from Frazier's, both agreed on the necessity of social change to end exploitation and bring about peaceful relations between the races.

Whereas Du Bois argued in favor of gradual transformation of social relations through reforms, Frazier opted for a more concrete assessment of the historical record and saw no other viable alternative to resolve the race question except through a radical transformation of the existing social-economic order. Thus Du Bois expected, earlier in the century, "changes to come mainly through reason, human sympathy, and the education of children" and "gravely doubt[ed] if, in the future, there will be any real recurrent necessity for upheaval."[24] However, the absence of any progress in race relations in subsequent decades led to his skepticism on the viability of this approach in the later years of his life, which, given his rejection of a revolutionary alternative to rejuvenate the movement, led him to political resignation and defeatism.

Frazier's stance was much more forceful and direct, allowing no pessimism of will or resolve. In contrast to Du Bois's reformist approach, Frazier argued that there could be "no fundamental changes in race relations . . . unless these changes are brought about in connection with some revolutionary movement."[25] However well intentioned, "the accumulation of goodwill will not do it," he added, because "the present racial situation is bound up with the present economic and social system."[26]

Advancing a reformist stance in line with the position of the National Association for the Advancement of Colored People (NAACP), with which he was associated for nearly twenty-five years,[27] Du Bois opted for limited political action within the established juridical boundaries of the system, instead of challenging it at its foundations. Although he expressed his skepticism with regard to the franchise as a way out of racial oppression, he advocated dissent through existing political channels, but remained indifferent to mass mobilization from below—a mobilization that was later successfully developed by more active leaders in the civil rights movement, such as Martin Luther King, Jr.

Frazier's views, however, were characteristically more radical and more militant, which pitted him and other activists against what he considered elitist intellectuals who stood apart from the masses and failed to take the necessary political steps to facilitate their liberation. This political divide helped fuel Frazier's views on the black upper and middle classes whom he despised as self-centered clones of their white counterparts, driven solely by their class interests.

While the changing class composition of the black community, which further intensified in the 1970s, gave rise to the subsequent debate on the caste and class controversy between William Julius Wilson, Charles Willie, and others in a different context,[28] Frazier's anticipation of the development of a new dynamic through the evolving contradictions of capitalist development in the late twentieth century led him to optimistic conclusions on the possibility of black-white unity within the working class, targeting the capitalists as the source of racial oppression and class exploitation—exploitation of an increasingly multiracial, multinational working class. Drawing his optimism on this score from the effects of the Great Depression on the working class in the 1930s and observing the "spread of radical ideas among working class Negroes through cooperation with white workers",[29] Frazier projected that "as the Negro may become an integral part of the proletariat, . . . the feeling against his color may break down in the face of a common foe."[30] Clarifying his position on the interplay of race, class, and social emancipation, "in the urban environment," he wrote, the black worker "is showing signs of understanding the struggle for power between the proletariat and the owning classes, and is beginning to cooperate with white workers in this struggle which offers the only hope of his complete emancipation."[31]

Despite their differences in political approach to the strategy and tactics of the struggle against racism and racial oppression, Du Bois and Frazier were two of the most prominent black intellectuals and social activists of the twentieth century; in their own distinct ways, they gave their utmost to this struggle and worked toward the building of a society based on equality among all citizens, regardless of race, gender, or class. In this sense, these two champions of human rights were among the pioneers of the modern civil rights movement that emerged toward the end of their lives. Yet, some three decades after their death, and nearly a century after the pronouncements of Du Bois on "the problem of the color line," racism and racial oppression continue to afflict American society. And in response to it, the fight against racism and for social justice continues to grow and intensify in these final years of the twentieth century.

Notes

[1] See James E. Blackwell and Morris Janowitz, eds., *Black Sociologists: Historical and Contemporary Perspectives* (Chicago: University of Chicago Press, 1974).

[2] W.E.B. Du Bois, in *The Atlantic Monthly* 87 (1901), 354.

[3] Meyer Weinberg, ed., *W.E.B. Du Bois: A Reader* (New York: Harper & Row, 1970), xv.

[4] John Milton Cooper, Jr., "Foreword," in Manning Marable, *W.E.B. Du Bois: Black Radical Democrat* (Boston: Twayne, 1986), vii.

[5] Herbert Aptheker, "W.E.B. Du Bois: Struggle Not Despair," *Clinical Sociology Review* 8 (1990): 62–63. For an extensive list of Du Bois's works, see Herbert Aptheker, *Annotated Bibliography of the Published Writings of W.E.B. Du Bois* (Millwood, N.Y.: Kraus-Thomson Organization, 1973).

[6] Anthony M. Platt, *E. Franklin Frazier Reconsidered* (New Brunswick, N.J.: Rutgers University Press, 1991), 3.

[7] Ibid.

[8] For an analysis of these developments, see E. Franklin Frazier, *Black Bourgeoisie* (Glencoe, Ill.: Free Press, 1957).

[9] W.E.B. Du Bois, "The White Masters of the World," in *The Writings of W.E.B. Du Bois*, ed. Virginia Hamilton (New York: Crowell, 1975), 201–2.

[10] W.E.B. Du Bois, "The Social Effects of Emancipation," in Weinberg, *W.E.B. Du Bois: A Reader*, 71.

[11] Ibid., 72.

[12] W.E.B. Du Bois, "The Class Struggle," in Weinberg, *W.E.B. Du Bois: A Reader*, 341.

[13] Ibid., 341.

[14] Ibid., 342–43.

[15] Du Bois, quoted in Gerald Horne, *Black & Red: W.E.B. Du Bois and the Afro-American Response to the Cold War, 1944–1963* (Albany: SUNY Press, 1986), 224.

[16] W.E.B. Du Bois, "Negroes and the Crisis of Capitalism in the United States," *Monthly Review* 4, no. 12 (April 1953): 482–83.

[17] Marable, *W.E.B. Du Bois*, 207.

[18] Horne, *Black & Red*, 225.

[19] Ibid., 224.

[20] For his earlier studies, see, for example, E. Franklin Frazier, *The Negro Family in the United States* (Chicago: University of Chicago Press, 1939). His later views on the relationship of race and class are developed in E. Franklin Frazier, *The Negro in the United States* (New York: Macmillan, 1949); and idem, *Race and Culture Contacts in the Modern World* (New York: Knopf, 1957).

[21] Platt, *E. Franklin Frazier Reconsidered*, 164.

[22] Frazier, quoted in ibid., 164.

[23] Ibid., 219.

[24] Du Bois, "The Class Struggle," in Weinberg, *W.E.B. Du Bois: A Reader*, 341.

[25] Frazier, quoted in Platt, *E. Franklin Frazier Reconsidered*, 186.

[26] Ibid.

[27] Du Bois was one of the principal founders of the NAACP in 1909 and for nearly twenty-five years served as editor of its official publication, *The Crisis*.

[28] This controversy, which began with the publication of William Julius Wilson's *The Declining Significance of Race* (Chicago: University of Chicago Press, 1978) and continued through his *The Truly Disadvantaged: The Inner City, the Underclass, and Public Policy* (Chicago: University of Chicago Press, 1987), took place within the context of the changing dynamics of the class structure within the black community resulting from the transformation of the U.S. economy and its impact on urban centers, which gave rise to an "underclass" of largely unemployed or menially employed black people trapped in America's inner cities. For an overview of the

different positions taken in this debate, see for example, Charles V. Willie, ed., *The Caste and Class Controversy on Race and Poverty* (Dix Hills, N.Y.: General Hall, 1989).

[29] Frazier, quoted in Platt, *E. Franklin Frazier Reconsidered*, 164.

[30] Ibid., 163.

[31] Ibid., 164.

PART II

CONTEMPORARY SOCIAL THEORY

| Chapter | **9** | **PARSONS, MERTON, AND FUNCTIONALIST THEORY** |

This chapter examines the central ideas presented in the works of Talcott Parsons, Robert K. Merton, and other functionalist theorists who came to dominate American sociology during the 1950s.[1] It critically analyzes their concept of human nature, social organization, and the social system.

Human Nature

In the process of development of a theory of social systems Parsons and other functionalists have made a number of assumptions about human nature. These assumptions constitute an integral part of contemporary functionalist theory. In this sense, the functionalist view of social organization, society, and the social system cannot be understood clearly unless we first comprehend the nature and theoretical underpinnings of these assumptions concerning the place of the individual in the social system.

In the Parsonian scheme, the basic alternatives that in certain combinations orient the individual actor to his or her culture and social system are referred to as the "pattern variables."[2] These are the dichotomies of (1) affectivity vs. affective neutrality, (2) self-orientation vs. collectivity orientation, (3) universalism vs. particularism, (4) achievement vs. ascription, and (5) specificity vs. diffuseness.[3] Parsons believes that the value orientation of the culture in which the individual finds himself or herself can be described in terms of these dichotomies. The individual learns this value orientation through the process of socialization and social control, which together facilitate the internalization of society's values. It is this internalization of value orientation patterns by individuals that keeps society going, according to Parsons.

Merton's approach to norms and values is likewise based on a process wherein an individual's values correspond to roles by way of "role performance."[4] Through this process, the person responds to other individuals only in terms of the defined expectations of acceptable behavior between them. Hence this near-mechanical view of individuals allows for the subsequent development of conformity and equilibrium.

Going beyond the traditional Parsonian frame of functional analysis and introducing into the model "middle range" theories that can be empirically examined, Merton has contributed an additional dimension to contemporary functionalist theory by identifying "manifest" and "latent" functions.[5] Manifest functions are those that are recognized and intended by the participants, whereas latent functions are those that are not recognized and have unintended consequences: "The distinction between manifest and latent functions was devised to preclude the inadvertent confusion, often found in the sociological literature, between conscious *motivations* for social behavior and its *objective consequences*."[6]

Thus while poverty in capitalist society is a deplorable condition of life for some (unemployed and poorly paid) segments of the population who find themselves in such a condition, it also serves as a latent function to justify the necessity for hard work so that employed workers continue to generate profits for their employers, with the threat that failing to do so would force them into unemployment and poverty. Hence, as in this case, latent functions are often the result of actions designed to benefit powerful social forces in society—forces that have an interest in securing conformity to the dominant values, ideas, and norms in society.

The individual, according to Parsons, Merton, and other functionalists, is built on the notion of conformity. Conformity of individuals is seen as crucial for the maintenance of the system. To illustrate this point clearly, Parsons explicitly states that

> the concept "integration" . . . is a mode of relation of the units of a system by virtue of which, on the one hand, they act so as collectively to avoid disrupting the system and making it impossible to maintain its stability, and, on the other hand, to "co-operate" to promote its functioning as a unity.[7]

Thus, "the well-integrated personality," writes Parsons,

feels an obligation to live up to expectations in his variously defined roles, to be a "good boy" to be a "good student," an "efficient worker," and so on. . . . The element of obligation in this sense is properly treated as "disinterested." It is a matter of "identification" with a generalized pattern, conformity with which is "right."[8]

According to the functionalist view, then, is that individuals acquire a sense of satisfaction when their behavior fulfills the expectations of the social group or society to which they belong and which sets the standards for individual behavior in varied social settings. As a result, the fulfillment of these goals becomes a motivational objective of individuals so that the resultant behavior is oriented toward the attainment of these goals. In this way, society achieves the integration of individuals into the social system and thereby secures social order and stability in the system. The crucial part in Parsons's system, then, is the internalization of value patterns by individuals in order to assure the maintenance of the social system. This internalization, Parsons argues, "constitutes the strategic element of [the] basic personality structure" because it is only in this way that social order can be obtained.[9]

Merton's equally central concern with conformity and integration leads him to observe that deviation from the norms established in society is a result of role or status strain or is a response to the divergence between socially established common goals and differentially distributed means. Acknowledging the prevalence and impact of such strains on society, Merton introduces into his model elements that are "dysfunctional" to the system.[10] Deviance is one such element that represents a dysfunctional relationship of the individual to society. If the deviance exceeds the acceptable range of tolerance and if the deviant cannot be persuaded to adopt an alternate role, the resultant variance and diversity within the social system creates the need for social control.[11] Thus, with the imposition of social control to maintain both the value patterns of a society as well as the motivation of its members, Parsons and Merton bring us full swing into their stable, functional social system.

Society and the Social System

The modern functionalists see society as a system of interdependent parts that are integrated through institutionalized norms and patterns of behavior.[12] Such integration, argues Parsons, assures the maintenance of the social system:

> Solidarity is the generalized capacity of agencies in the society to "bring into line" the behavior of system units in accordance with the integrative needs of the system, to check or reverse disruptive tendencies to deviant behavior, and to promote the conditions of harmonious cooperation.[13]

Thus the functionalist view of society is concerned with the relationship of equilibrating forces between the various parts of the system. As each part or unit of the system is given equal importance, any change in one part will affect all the others. To maintain conditions of stability within the system, society must be in a state of "equilibrium"—one that promotes the survival and maintenance of the prevailing social system. Such rationalization, however, has led critics to charge that modern functionalist theory legitimizes mid-twentieth-century dominant capitalist ideology. Indeed, this is clearly evident in their discussion of social classes, politics, and the state.

Generally, the functionalists see social classes and class inequality as naturally occuring phenomena in all societies at all times. In their classic essay, "Some Principles of Stratification," Kingsley Davis and Wilbert Moore speak of "the *universal necessity* which calls forth stratification in *any* social system."[14] Moreover, "the main functional necessity explaining the universal presence of stratification," write Davis and Moore, "is precisely the *requirement* faced by *any* society of placing and motivating individuals in the social structure."[15]

> Inevitably, then, a society must have, first, some kind of rewards that it can use as inducements, and second, some way of distributing these rewards differentially according to positions. The rewards and their distribu-

tion become a part of the social order, and thus give rise
to stratification.[16]

This is so, Davis and Moore categorically state, in "every society, no
matter how simple or complex."[17]

Such an assertion, however, is based on the functionalist
(ideological) assumption that stratification is "functionally necessary" to ensure *the maintenance of the existing social system* and not
a scientific analysis of historical reality. "Functional theories,"
comments Arthur Stinchcombe, "are like other scientific theories:
they have empirical consequences which are either true or false.
Deciding whether they are true or false is not a theoretical or
ideological matter but an empirical one."[18] As wealth of data avail-
able on a large number of primitive societies show, almost all (98
percent) of hunting and gathering (primitive communal) societies do
not have a class system or structured social inequality, while the
remaining 2 percent have become "stratified" as a result of contact
with more advanced societies.[19] Hence, as humans have lived in
primitive hunting and gathering societies as the predominant form
of social organization for most of human history, it is clear that the
historical evolution of homosapiens for thousands of years has been
unquestionably highly democratic and egalitarian. Only in more
recent times do we begin to see the development of class systems,
hence of class inequality.[20]

To his credit, Melvin M. Tumin, a functionalist himself, has
expressed strong criticism of the Davis-Moore thesis, refuting the
latter's contentions on inequality and stratification. In fact, Tumin's
critical analysis of the problem leads him to reach almost exactly the
opposite conclusions from those of Davis and Moore, as he specifies
various "negative functions, or dysfunctions, of institutionalized
social inequality," such as "human ignorance, war, poverty."[21]
Responding to the Davis-Moore thesis on the functional necessity of
inequality, Tumin raises some important issues that challenge this
view. He writes:

> Since a theoretical model *can* be devised in which all
> other clearly indispensable major social functions are
> performed, but in which inequality as motive and reward

is absent, how then account for stratification in terms of structural and functional necessities and inevitablities?[22]

Extending his analysis to account for the key mechanism that perpetuates structured social inequality, "an essential characteristic of all known kinship systems," writes Tumin,

> is that they function as transmitters of inequalities from generation to generation. Similarly, an essential characteristic of all known stratification systems is that they employ the kinship system as their agent of transmission of inequalities.
>
> To the extent that this is true, then it is true by definition that the elimination from kinship systems of their function as transmitters of inequalities (and hence the alteration of the definition of kinship systems) would eliminate those inequalities which were generation-linked.
>
> Obviously, the denial to parents of their ability and right to transmit both advantages and disadvantages to their offspring would require a fundamental alteration in all existing concepts of kinship structure. At the least, there would have to be a vigilant separation maintained between the unit which reproduces and the unit which socializes, maintains and places. In theory, this separation is eminently possible. In practice, it would be revolutionary.[23]

Indeed it would! By curbing the transfer of wealth and property through the alteration of the nature and function of the kinship structure, it is indeed possible to bring up a new generation of individuals without the necessity of a significant level of social inequality.

Power, Politics, and the State

Turning to politics, Parsons and other contemporary functionalists have characterized the modern U.S. state as a democratic institution whose primary function is to secure order within the system.[24] Representing the interests of society as a whole, the state coordinates the other major institutions of society—economic, educational, religious, and so on—and advances both the general social welfare and that of the individuals within it. Thus, for the functionalists, while the state provides strong, effective leadership and represents institutionalized power and authority vis-à-vis individual citizens, its actions reflect widespread and diverse interests that exist in society—interests that the functionalists claim are well represented within the state. As the supreme guardian of "representative democracy," the state thus fulfills its role in carrying out its social tasks while ensuring its democratic control by society.

"Power," writes Parsons, "is a generalized facility or resource in the society":

> It has to be divided or allocated, but it also has to be produced and it has collective as well as distributive functions. It has the capacity to mobilize the resources of the society for the attainment of goals for which a general "public" commitment has been made, or may be made. It is mobilization, above all, of the action of persons and groups, which is *binding* on them by virtue of their position in the society.[25]

Thus the state maintains an autonomous role for itself as the sole public authority and at the same time assures the equal distribution of power across competing political groups in society. "This tension in functionalist thinking on the state between a view of the necessity for a strong, modernizing, central co-ordinator on the one hand, and a relatively equal distribution of social powers on the other," observes one critic, "reflects the cross-pulls from two allegedly functional pre-requisites: the need for autonomy and the need for integration."[26] By distributing its control among a broad range of social groups and preventing its monopolization by any one group, the state, according to the functionalists, thus paves the way for political competition and "pluralist democracy."[27]

Empirical reality, however, is much different from what contemporary functionalists would have us believe. While functionalists such as Robin Williams argue that "no 'rule by monopoly' is in sight in the American economy" and "corporate shares are held by large numbers of individuals," and further, that the American pattern of power distribution is "the balancing of interests and compromising of conflicts through multiple power-centers, numerous separate channels of influence, and the subdivision of political authorities,"[28] the true extent of wealth/ownership and of political power can be illustrated as follows: the top 10 percent of American families own 78 percent of real estate, 90 percent of all publicly held corporate stocks, 90 percent of all bonds, and 94 percent of net business assets.[29] Moreover, the top one-half of 1 percent of all families own nearly half of all corporate stocks and bonds, and nearly two-thirds of all business assets.[30] Further, the two hundred largest U.S. corporations, many of which are mutually controlled through interlocking directorates, control more than 75 percent of all corporately held assets and account for nearly two-thirds of total net profits.[31]

Conclusion

The functionalist conception of human nature, society, and politics examined in this chapter reveals that contemporary functionalists have uncritically accepted existing structures and conditions of capitalist society as givens and have thus contributed, implicitly or explicitly, toward the maintenance of the existing social order and the perpetuation of dominant capitalist ideology. This has opened the way to a barrage of criticism of modern functionalism for being nothing more than an ideological expression of the capitalist system in the United States.

The functionalist contention that in America political power resides with many diverse and equally powerful groups reflecting the interests of the vast majority of the population has similarly come under strong criticism in recent decades. In the late 1950s, critics, led by C. Wright Mills, began to provide a powerful critique of Parsonian functionalism that set the stage for subsequent debates within sociology. Expanding this effort during the 1960s and 1970s, G. William Domhoff and numerous other critical sociologists were instrumental in widening the critique of modern functionalism and thus breaking its decades-long monopoly over social theory.

It is through such critique of the ideological implications of modern functionalist theory vis-à-vis its earlier intellectual hegemony within sociology that more and more sociologists have come to understand clearly the dynamics of recent developments in contemporary sociological theory. The contributions to this critique through alternative theoretical formulations of the American social reality provided by Mills and Domhoff are discussed in the next two chapters.

Notes

[1] Although this chapter addresses two different versions of contemporary functionalist theory—Parsonian and Mertonian, or what C. Wright Mills called "Grand Theory" and "Abstracted Empiricism," respectively—we use the term "functionalism" when referring to both versions.

[2] Talcott Parsons, *The Social System* (New York: Free Press, 1951), 67.

[3] Ibid.

[4] Robert K. Merton, *Social Theory and Social Structure* (New York: Free Press, 1968), 390–94.

[5] Ibid., 114–18.

[6] Ibid., 114.

[7] Parsons, *Essays in Sociological Theory*, rev. ed. (Glencoe, Ill.: Free Press, 1954), 71.

[8] Ibid., 56–57.

[9] Parsons, *The Social System*, 228.

[10] Merton, *Social Theory and Social Structure*, 105.

[11] Ibid., 230–48.

[12] Harry M. Johnson, *Sociology: A Systematic Introduction* (New York: Harcourt, Brace, 1960).

[13] Talcott Parsons, cited in Chandler Morse, "The Functional Imperatives," in *The Social Theories of Talcott Parsons*, ed. Max Black (Englewood Cliffs, N.J.: Prentice Hall, 1961), 126.

[14] Kingsley Davis and Wilbert E. Moore, "Some Principles of Stratification," *American Sociological Review* 10, no. 2 (April 1945): 242.

[15] Ibid.

[16] Ibid., 243.

[17] Ibid.

[18] Arthur L. Stinchcombe, "Some Empirical Consequences of the Davis–Moore Theory of Stratification," *American Sociological Review* 28 (October 1963): 808.

[19] Gerhard Lenski, *Power and Privilege* (New York: McGraw-Hill, 1966); Eleanor B. Leacock, "Introduction," in F. Engels, *The Origin of the Family, Private Property, and the State* (New York: International Publishers, 1972).

[20] See Albert Szymanski, *Class Structure* (New York: Praeger, 1983), chap. 2.

[21] Melvin Tumin, "Some Principles of Stratification: A Critical Analysis," *American Sociological Review* 18, no. 4 (August 1953): 394; and idem, "Reply to Kingsley Davis," *American Sociological Review* 18, no. 6 (December 1953): 672.

[22] Tumin, "Reply to Kingsley Davis," 672.

[23] Ibid.

[24] Talcott Parsons, *Societies: An Evolutionary Approach* (Englewood Cliffs, N.J.: Prentice Hall, 1966); and idem, "On the Concept of Political Power," in T. Parsons, *Sociological Theory and Modern Society* (New York: Free Press, 1967).

[25] Talcott Parsons, *Structure and Process in Modern Societies* (New York: Free Press, 1960), 221.

[26] Roger King, *The State in Modern Society* (Chatham, N.J.: Chatham House, 1986), 15.

[27] S.N. Eisenstadt, ed., *Modernization: Protest and Change* (Englewood Cliffs, N.J.: Prentice Hall, 1966) cited in King, *The State in Modern Society*, 15.

[28] Ibid.

[29] Jerry Kloby, "Increasing Class Polarization in the United States: The Growth of Wealth and Income Inequality," in *Critical Perspectives in Sociology*, ed. Berch Berberoglu (Dubuque, Iowa: Kendall/Hunt, 1991), 44.

[30] Ibid.

[31] U.S. Bureau of the Census, *Statistical Abstract of the United States, 1990* (Washington, D.C.: Government Printing Office, 1990), 541.

10 MILLS ON THE POWER
ELITE AND THE
MILITARY ASCENDANCY

One of the earliest and most powerful critics of Parsons and'
structural functionalism in American sociology was C. Wright
Mills. Challenging the domain assumptions of the discipline sus-
tained by the functionalist mainstream in the conservative 1950s,
Mills soon became one of the most outspoken and controversial
social theorists of the postwar period in the United States. Taking on
the discipline's domain assumptions singlehandedly, Mills called
for the unleashing of "the sociological imagination" to untangle
some of the most critical issues of our time—power, politics, and
society.[1]

Writing at the height of the Cold War and the McCarthy witch
hunts of the 1950s, Mills provided a devastating critique of establishment sociology by launching an all-out attack on Parsonian
functionalism, which had played an important role in rationalizing
the status quo and thereby promoting the existing social order and
reinforcing unequal power relations in society.

This chapter examines the ideas of Mills on the American power
structure that he developed as a critique of pluralism. Focusing on
his analysis of power relations at the highest levels of American
society, the chapter provides a critical overview of his concept of
political power, which he presented as an important corrective to the
conservative theories of Parsons and what came to be known as
Parsonian sociology.

The Power Elite

Influenced by Weber, Mosca, Pareto, and Marx, Mills developed an
institutional theory of political power, one based on an articulation
of the combined expression of a "power elite." Rejecting the Marxist
contention that the capitalist class through its control of the govern-

ment is also a *ruling* class,[2] Mills adopted an institutional approach, believing that power had shifted from owners of the means of production (or capitalists) to managers and functionaries of the key institutions of American society—the economy, the polity, and, especially, the military.

Such a view forced Mills to focus on high-ranking individual policymakers, especially generals and admirals, whom he considered as part of the higher circles that make up the "power elite":

> Within American society, major national power now resides in the economic, the political, and the military domains. . . . As each of these domains has coincided with the others, as decisions tend to become total in their consequence, *the leading men* in each of the three domains of power—*the warlords, the corporation chieftains, the political directorate*—tend to come together, to form the power elite of America.[3]

The power elite, Mills continues, is composed of those who are "in command of the major hierarchies and organizations of modern society":

> They rule the big corporations. They run the machinery of the state and claim its prerogatives. They direct the military establishment. They occupy the strategic command posts of the social structure.[4]

"The power to make decisions of national and international consequence," Mills points out,

> is now so clearly seated in political, military, and economic institutions that other areas of society seem off to the side. . . . The scattered institutions of religion, education and family are increasingly shaped by the big three, in which history-making decisions now regularly occur. . . . This triangle of power is now a structural fact, and it is the key to any understanding of the higher circles in America today.[5]

The critical point in Mills's analysis of the power elite is not the mere identification of the elite in the three key institutions that constitute the American power structure but the interrelationship between these institutions and between members of the elite that control and direct them:

> The shape and meaning of the power elite today can be understood only when these three sets of structural trends are seen at their point of coincidence. . . . Accordingly, at the top of this structure, the power elite has been shaped by the coincidence of interest between . . . the professional politicians . . . the corporate chieftains and the professional warlords.[6]

The interrelationship between these institutions and between their top leadership is such that retired generals become corporate executives and serve on the boards of directors of large corporations that sell inflated military hardware through lucrative defense contracts signed by old associates in the military, while corporate executives who enter politics serve the interests of big business once they hold key government posts that facilitate the passage of legislation favorable to corporate interests. Thus, as the linkage between big business and the government becomes consolidated, so too the control of the state by business interests becomes solidified, thereby diminishing the prospects for open discussion and debate on public policy:

> The shift of corporation men into the political directorate has accelerated the decline of the politicians in the Congress to the middle levels of power; the formation of the power elite rests in part upon this relegation. It rests also upon the increased official secrecy behind which great decisions are made without benefit of public or even of Congressional debate.[7]

The Rise of the Military

Corresponding to the increased influence over and control of the government by big business, Mills also saw the rise of the military and its more direct role and influence in political affairs, as exemplified by General Dwight D. Eisenhower's ascendance to the presidency in the 1950s. "In so far as the structural clue to the power elite today lies in the enlarged and military state," writes Mills, "that clue becomes evident in the military ascendancy."[8] In a chapter of *The Power Elite* titled "The Military Ascendancy," Mills points out: "As the United States has become a great world power, the military establishment has expanded, and members of its higher echelons have moved directly into diplomatic and political circles."[9] Moreover, "the military order, once a slim establishment in a context of civilian distrust, has become the largest and most expensive feature of government."[10]

> The high military have gained decisive political and economic relevance. The seemingly permanent military threat places a premium upon them and virtually all political and economic actions are now judged in terms of military definitions of reality: the higher military have ascended to a firm position within the power elite of our time.[11]

The ascendancy of the military goes far beyond the institutional boundaries of the political and economic order, according to Mills. The military establishment, he argues, is attempting to extend its power into the civilian sphere by molding public opinion in favor of a military definition of reality:

> It is not only within the higher political and economic, scientific and educational circles that the military ascendancy is apparent. . . .
> The military manipulation of civilian opinion and the military invasion of the civilian mind are now important ways in which the power of the warlords is steadily exerted.[12]

The increasing power of the military (and its top leadership) in civilian affairs, Mills contends, "points to the tendency of military men . . . to pursue ends of their own, and to turn other institutional areas into means for accomplishing them."[13] As a result, since World

War II, he argues, "those who command the enlarged means of American violence have come to possess considerable autonomy, as well as great influence, among their political and economic colleagues."[14] The generals, he adds, "are now more powerful than they have ever been in the history of the American elite; they have now more means of exercising power in many areas of American life which were previously civilian domains."[15]

Conclusion

The close association of big business, the government, and the military, and between the heads of each of these institutions, led Mills to conclude that, together, this collection of powerful men constitutes the center of power in American society, with the military, through its direct presence in the executive branch, wielding a disproportionate power stemming from the entry of the Pentagon into power politics.

Developments since 1960, however, have shown that the prominence of the military in politics was in effect an outcome of postwar popular sentiment toward a general (Eisenhower) who led the United States to victory in World War II, than the rise of the military, as such, to the center stage of power politics, as Mills's empiricist observations led him to believe. Critics have pointed out that, all appearances to the contrary, his exaggerated emphasis on the rise of the military—hence his (unwarranted) attribution of extraordinary powers to the "warlords," which they contend the latter lacked—has had a lopsided effect on Mills's tripartite model of the power elite.[16] Countering Mills's argument on this point, G. William Domhoff, for example, has pointed out that

> if the United States in the postwar era has adopted what Mills called a military definition of reality, it is because this was chosen by leading big business members of the power elite on the basis of their understanding of national goals and international events, not because it was somehow foisted on them by the military.[17]

A more serious criticism of Mills, brought out in subsequent work on the U.S. power structure launched by Domhoff and others in the 1960s, is the absence in Mills's analysis of a connection between the power elite and what Domhoff has called "the social upper class."[18] Herbert Aptheker, for example, has pointed out that Mills's

> projection of the concept of a triangular power elite, which he explicitly offers in preference to that of a ruling class, is based on a misconception of "ruling class." Moreover, in his tripartite division of the wielders of control he avoids comparing the relative weight of each of the three and tends to ignore the central depository of power—the financial overlords.[19]

This misconception of the *source* of power in American society prevented the development of a structural analysis of power linked to *class* until Domhoff introduced into the discussion the central role of the "upper class" in government through the former's transformation from a cohesive social-economic class into a "governing class," a topic we address in the next chapter.

Notes

[1] See C. Wright Mills, *The Sociological Imagination* (New York: Oxford University Press, 1959); and idem, *The Power Elite* (New York: Oxford University Press, 1956). See also C. Wright Mills, *White Collar: The American Middle Classes* (New York: Oxford University Press, 1951).

[2] Mills, *The Power Elite*, 277.

[3] Ibid., 6, 9; emphasis added.

[4] Ibid., 4.

[5] C. Wright Mills, "The Structure of Power in American Society," in *Power, Politics, and People: The Collected Essays of C. Wright Mills*, ed. Irving Louis Horowitz (New York: Oxford University Press, 1963), 27.

[6] Mills, *The Power Elite*, 276.

[7] Mills, "The Structure of Power in American Society," 35.

[8] Mills, *The Power Elite*, 275.

[9] Ibid., 202.

[10] Mills, "The Structure of Power in American Society," 28.

[11] Ibid.

[12] Mills, *The Power Elite*, 219, 221–22.

[13] Ibid., 222.

[14] Ibid., 202.

[15] Ibid.

[16] See G. William Domhoff and Hoyt B. Ballard, eds. *C. Wright Mills and the Power Elite* (Boston: Beacon Press, 1969).

[17] G. William Domhoff, *The Higher Circles: The Governing Class in America* (New York: Vintage, 1971), 139.

[18] For an extended discussion on this point, see the next chapter.

[19] Herbert Aptheker, *The World of C. Wright Mills* (New York: Marzani and Munsell, 1960), 19–20.

Chapter	**11**	**DOMHOFF ON THE POWER STRUCTURE AND THE GOVERNING CLASS**

Taking Mills's analysis of the American power structure one step further, G. William Domhoff has made an important contribution to our understanding of the social basis of political power by linking the upper class to the major political institutions of American society, especially the state—a relationship embodied in the concept of the "governing class."[1]

This chapter examines the ideas of Domhoff on the American power structure, which he, like Mills, developed as a critique of pluralist theory. Examining his analysis of the governing class in America, the chapter provides a critical overview of his concept of political power in America that goes beyond Mills's characterization of the power elite.

The Power Structure

In his now classic *Who Rules America?* Domhoff took a giant step forward beyond Mills's pioneering study of the power elite by looking behind the movers and shapers of American domestic and foreign policy. Attempting to understand the common interests of the leading forces of the power structure and their connection to the social upper class of wealthy owners of the giant corporations, Domhoff discovered that through a multitude of political processes the upper class has come directly and indirectly to dominate the government and has become a ruling, or governing, class.

Clarifying the meaning of the concepts of "power elite," "upper class," and "governing class," Domhoff makes explicit his own analysis of the Americal power structure and thus sets himself apart from that developed by Mills. The "power elite," Domhoff points out, "encompasses all those who are in command positions in institutions controlled by members of the upper (governing) class."[2] In this sense, Domhoff's definition of the power elite is similar to

Mills's concept, that is, an elite made up of the top functionaries of the leading institutions of American society, but goes beyond Mills's tripartite model of power, in that Domhoff differentiates the position of the power elite from that of the upper class. Referring to the former, "This power elite," Domhoff argues, "is the *leadership group* of the upper class as a whole,"

> but it is *not the same thing as the upper class,* for not all members of the upper class are members of the power elite and not all members of the power elite are part of the upper class. It is members of the power elite who take part in the processes that maintain the class structure.[3]

What distinguishes Domhoff's approach from that of Mills is Domhoff's focus on the central problematic of "whether or not the institution [that the power elite serves] is *controlled by members of the upper class,*"[4] for it is this *class control* that is decisive, *not* the particular characteristics or motives of the power elite per se, as Mills had emphasized. "Thus, if we can show that members of the upper class," Domhoff continues,

> control the corporations through stock ownership and corporate directorships, the military through the Department of Defense, and the corporate law profession through large corporate law firms and major law schools, we will have gone a long way toward demonstrating that *the aims of the American power elite,* as defined by either Mills or this book, *are necessarily those of members of the upper class.*[5]

Domhoff defines the upper class as a social class "made up of rich businessmen and their families" and points out that it is

> closely knit by such institutions as stock ownership, trust funds, intermarriages, private schools, exclusive city clubs, exclusive summer resorts, debutante parties, foxhunts, charity drives, and, last but not least, corporation boards.[6]

In short, the upper class, Domhoff points out, is based on "great wealth and unique life styles of intermarrying and interacting families of high social standing."[7] After a detailed examination of the position and connections of the wealthy in America, Domhoff concludes: "There is in the United States an intermarrying social upper class, based upon business wealth, that has a rather definite set of boundaries which are guarded by . . . exclusive institutions.[8]

Going a step further, Domhoff raises the central question of his inquiry: "Is this social upper class, with its several institutional focal points and its several means of assimilating new members, also a 'governing class'?"[9] And, if so, what is the process by which the American upper class becomes a national governing class?

The Upper Class as Governing Class

In both *Who Rules America?* and *The Higher Circles: The Governing Class in America*, Domhoff documents how the upper class is in fact a cohesive social class based on the ownership of the large corporations and banks and that this class, through its control of numerous private and public institutions, has become a "governing class."[10] Defining the governing class as

> a social upper class which owns a disproportionate amount of the country's wealth, receives a disproportionate share of the country's yearly income, contributes a disproportionate number of its members to governmental bodies and decision-making groups, and dominates the policy-forming process through a variety of means[11]

Domhoff goes on to show how, through numerous institutional mechanisms, the social upper class becomes a bona fide governing class.

After extensive study and analysis of the relationship between the upper class, the power elite, and the key governmental institutions of American society, Domhoff concludes: "Members of the American upper class and their employees control the Executive branch of the federal government, . . . the Judicial branch and the regulatory agencies," including "the military, the CIA, and the FBI."[12] Moreover, the upper class is well represented in and has substantial influence over the legislative branch and has an impact on other key institutions, including universities, foundations, clubs, advisory councils, and numerous other organizations.[13] Through this control and domination of the key governmental and social institutions of American society, the upper class has become a governing class, according to Domhoff.

From Governing Class to Ruling Class

Whereas Domhoff had in his earlier work avoided the use of the term "ruling class" because, as he put it, it is "a term that implies a Marxist view of history"[14] (with which he apparently did not want to be identified), opting instead for "the more neutral term 'governing class,'"[15] in his later works—beginning with *The Powers That Be: Processes of Ruling Class Domination in America*—he drops the term "governing class" and substitutes in its place the concept of the "ruling class"—a concept he had rejected a decade earlier.[16]

In the opening chapter of *The Powers That Be*, titled "The Ruling Class and the Problem of Power," Domhoff defines the term "ruling class" as follows:

> By a ruling class I mean a clearly demarcated social class which has "power" over the government (state apparatus) and underlying population within a given nation (state). Evidence for the "power" of a ruling class can be found in such indicators as:
> 1. A disproportionate amount of wealth and income as compared to other social classes and groups within the state;
> 2. A higher standing than other social classes within the state on a variety of well-being statistics;
> 3. Control over the major social and economic institutions of the state;
> 4. Domination over the governmental processes of the country.[17]

In a broader sense, then, the "ruling class is a social class that subordinates other social classes to its own profit or advantage"[18] and dominates the major institutions of society, especially the state, to advance its class interests.

Differentiating his concept of the "ruling class" from Mills's "power elite," Domhoff writes: "C. Wright Mills first introduced the concept of a power elite into the sociological literature as a substitute for 'ruling class.'"[19] In contrast, Domhoff states:

> I define the power elite as the leadership group or *operating arm* of the ruling class. It is made up of active, working members of the ruling class and high-level employees in institutions controlled by members of the ruling class.[20]

"The difference between Mills' definition and mine," Domhoff continues, "lies in the fact that"

> (1) I do not assume *a priori* that any institutionally based group is by definition part of the power elite, as Mills did in so designating leaders within corporate, military and governmental bureaucracies; and (2) I have grounded the power elite in a social class. Using this approach, it is possible to determine empirically which parts of the economy and government can be considered direct outposts of the ruling class by virtue of disproportionate participation by members of the power elite.[21]

"Both of these concepts—ruling class and power elite," Domhoff concludes, "are important in an examination of how America is ruled, for they bring together the class-rule and institutional-elite perspectives" of power in American society.[22]

Conclusion

Despite his significant contribution to power-structure research and substantial improvement over Mills's concept of the power elite, Domhoff has been criticized for paying insufficient attention to class relations and class struggle beyond the instrumental identification of control of the state and other institutions of American society by the governing (or ruling) upper class. Marxist critics have faulted him for having focused too much on the institutional aspects of the policy-formation process and for ignoring a class analysis of the capitalist political economy that incorporates a dialectical approach to class. Moreover, Domhoff's loose usage of the term "upper class" has led to further criticism of his overall model, which he has built outside the Marxist problematic of the ruling *capitalist* class.

While Domhoff in his latest book, *The Power Elite and the State*, attempts to correct this shortcoming by injecting an element of class analysis into his new theory of power and the state, he, like Mills, continues to reject Marxist theories of the state and opts instead for an eclectic-empiricist approach in line with his previous studies of power in the United States.[23] Thus, although he clearly states that "the relationship between states and social classes [is] the crucial issue of this book," Domhoff criticizes the efforts of the structural Marxists by asserting that "they abandoned the study of social power in general for more narrow concerns such as 'class structure' or 'state power.'"[24] Rejecting the Marxist approach and anticipating criticisms of the eclectic theoretical position he has come to adopt in his studies of the U.S. power structure during the past twenty-five years, Domhoff admits:

> After all those years spent wandering in the empirical wilderness, surrounded on every side by pluralists, structural Marxists, and utility maximizers . . . I hope the eclecticism of my view . . . does not continue to create confusion for the pigeonholers, taxonomists, and single-cause theorists who now dominate discussions of power in America.[25]

Domhoff's objections to structural Marxism notwithstanding, to develop a more comprehensive understanding of the relationship between class, power, and the state, we turn in the next chapter to the debate on the theory of the capitalist state—a debate that has taken center stage in Marxist circles during the past two decades.

Notes

[1] See G. William Domhoff, *Who Rules America?* (Englewood Cliffs, N.J.: Prentice Hall, 1967); and idem, *The Higher Circles: The Governing Class in America* (New York: Vintage, 1971). For the relationship of Domhoff's work to that of Mills, see G. William Domhoff and Hoyt B. Ballard, eds., *C. Wright Mills and the Power Elite* (Boston: Beacon Press, 1968).

[2] Domhoff, *Who Rules America?* 10.

[3] G. William Domhoff, *Who Rules America Now?* (New York: Simon & Schuster, 1983), 2.

[4] Domhoff, *Who Rules America?* 10; emphasis added.

[5] Ibid.

[6] Ibid., 4.

[7] Domhoff, *The Higher Circles*, 32.

[8] Domhoff, *Who Rules America?*, 33.

[9] Ibid., 5.

[10] See Domhoff, *The Higher Circles*, 103–9 and idem, *Who Rules America?* 156. See also G. William Domhoff, *The Powers That Be: The Processes of Ruling Class Domination in America* (New York: Vintage, 1979), chap. 1.

[11] Domhoff, *The Higher Circles*, 109.

[12] Domhoff, *Who Rules America?* 84, 131.

[13] Domhoff, *Who Rules America Now?* chaps. 4 and 5.

[14] Domhoff, *Who Rules America?* 3.

[15] Ibid.

[16] See Domhoff, *The Powers That Be*.

[17] Ibid., 12.

[18] Ibid., 13.

[19] Ibid., 13–14.

[20] Ibid. 13; emphasis added.

[21] Ibid., 14.

[22] Ibid., 14–15.

[23] See G. William Domhoff, *The Power Elite and the State* (New York: Aldine de Gruyter, 1990).

[24] Ibid., xviii, 7. Domhoff writes: "I believe that the Marxian analysis of the state in democratic capitalist societies is wrong because it incorporates a false homology between the economy and the state that distorts its view of the state and creates a tendency to downplay the importance of representative democracy." Ibid., 8.

[25] Ibid., xix, 14–15.

Chapter 12 ALTHUSSER, POULANTZAS, AND MILIBAND ON POLITICS AND THE STATE

This chapter focuses on the views of three contemporary Marxist theorists—Louis Althusser, Nicos Poulantzas, and Ralph Miliband— on politics and the state in capitalist society. Concerned with the base-superstructure problematic and the nature and role of the capitalist state, these theorists provide us with the framework for an informed analysis of the debates on the state and politics in late capitalist society.

Ideology and the Political Superstructure

In the late 1960s, Louis Althusser reintroduced into Marxist discourse Lenin's and Gramsci's contributions on ideology and the state and provided an extended discussion on the basic concepts of historical materialism. Althusser played a key role in the effort to revitalize critical thought on the subject through the incorporation of the Gramscian notion of ideological hegemony into his own analysis of "ideological state apparatuses."[1]

In linking the political superstructure to the social-economic base, or mode of production, Althusser argued in favor of the classical Marxist position, which identifies the superstructure as determined "in the last instance" by the base: "The upper floors," he wrote, in reference to the political superstructure, "could not 'stay up' (in the air) alone, if they did not rest precisely on their base."[2] Thus the state, the supreme political institution and repressive apparatus of society, "enables the ruling classes to ensure their domination over the working class, thus enabling the former to subject the latter to the process of surplus-value extortion."[3] This is so precisely because the state is controlled by the ruling class. And such control makes the state, and the superstructure in general, dependent on, and determined by, the dominant class in the base.

111

In his essay "Ideology and Ideological State Apparatuses," Althusser expands his analysis of the base-superstructure relationship to include other superstructural institutions—cultural, religious, educational, legal, and so on. As the hegemony of the ruling class in these spheres becomes critical for its control over the dominated classes, and society in general, the class struggle takes on a three-tiered attribute, consisting of the economic, political, and ideological levels. Central to the process of ruling-class ideological domination is the installation by the ruling class of the dominant ideology in the ideological state apparatuses, according to Althusser.

> The ideology of the ruling class does not become the ruling ideology by virtue of the seizure of state power alone. It is by the installation of the ideological state apparatuses in which this ideology is realized itself that it becomes the ruling ideology.[4]

The relationship between ruling-class domination and the dominant ideology is also emphasized by Poulantzas, who further developed Althusser's conceptualization of ideology, situating it in the context of class domination and class struggle. "The dominant ideology, by assuring the practical insertion of agents in the social structure," Poulantzas points out, "aims at the maintenance (the cohesion) of the structure, and this means *above all* class domination and exploitation."[5]

> It is precisely in this way that within a social formation ideology is dominated by the ensemble of representations, values, notions, beliefs, etc. by means of which class domination is perpetuated: in other words it is dominated by what can be called the ideology of the dominant class.[6]

This Althusserian conception of the relationship between the base and the superstructure, especially the state and the ideological state apparatuses, came to inform Poulantzas's analysis of classes, class struggle, and the state and set the stage for the recent discussion and debate on the Marxist theory of the state.

The Poulantzas-Miliband Debate on the Capitalist State

The Poulantzas-Miliband debate on the nature and role of the capitalist state in the early 1970s prompted renewed interest in Marxist theorizing on the capitalist state during the past two decades.[7] In this debate, one position emphasized the direct and indirect control of the state by the dominant capitalist class, and another emphasized the structural imperatives of the capitalist system affecting the state and its "relative autonomy." These two views correspond to the so-called "instrumentalist" and "structuralist" positions associated with Ralph Miliband and Nicos Poulantzas, respectively. Central to the debate are questions related to the class nature of the state, the relationship between different classes and the state, and the notion of relative autonomy in the exercise of state power.[8]

In his original formulation of the problem in *The State in Capitalist Society*, Miliband approaches the question of the state via a critique of the pluralist models still dominant in political sociology and mainstream political theory. In so doing, he provides an approach and analysis that earns his work the unwarranted label "instrumentalism." And it is in reaction to this instrumentalism that critiques of his work have resulted in the formulation of a counterposition that has come to be labeled "structuralism."

The central question addressed in the initial formulation of the instrumentalist problematic has been a determination of the role of the state in a society dominated by capitalist social relations. In this context, Miliband's study of the capitalist state focuses on the special relationship between the state and the capitalist class, and the mechanisms of control of the state by this class that de facto transform the state into a *capitalist state.*

In contrast, Poulantzas, representing the so-called structuralist position, focuses on the structural constraints of the capitalist system that set limits to the state's autonomy and force it to work within the framework of an order that yields results invariably favorable to the dominant capitalist class. According to this view, it is by virtue of the system of production itself in capitalist society that the state becomes a *capitalist* state, even in the absence of direct control of the state apparatus by capitalists.

It should be pointed out, however, that the degree of lack of direct control of the state apparatus by the capitalist class determines the degree of the state's relative autonomy from this class. And this relative autonomy in turn gives the state the necessary freedom to manage the overall interests of the capitalist class and rule society on behalf of the established capitalist order.

The central problem for these competing views of the state is not so much whether the state in capitalist society is a *capitalist* state—they agree that it is—but *how* that state *becomes* a capitalist state. Far more than the limited academic value, the answers to this question have immense political implications because the debates surrounding this issue originally emerged in Europe in response to the pivotal political question regarding the strategy and tactics of taking state power under advanced capitalism.

Instrumentalism versus Structuralism

Let us briefly look at the fundamentals of the instrumentalist versus structuralist problematic and show, in the process, that the dichotomy has been ill conceived, as both Miliband and Poulantzas ultimately, in later reformulation of their positions, basically accept the validity of their critics' conclusions.

To start with, in his initial formulation of the problem, Miliband writes:

> In the Marxist scheme, the "ruling class" of capitalist society is that class which owns and controls the means of production and which is able, by virtue of the economic power thus conferred upon it, to use the state as its instrument for the domination of society.[9]

This seemingly instrumentalist statement is expounded by Miliband through his focus on "patterns and consequences of personal and social ties between individuals occupying positions of power in different institutional spheres."[10] Concentrating on a study of the nature of the capitalist class, the mechanisms that tie this class to the state, and the specific relationships between state policies and class interests,[11] Miliband leaves himself open to charges of voluntarism and instrumentalism.

In contrast, Poulantzas argues that "the *direct* participation of members of the capitalist class in the state apparatus and in the government, even where it exists, is not the important side of the matter."[12] What is crucial to understand, according to Poulantzas, is this:

> The relation between the bourgeois class and the state is an *objective relation.* This means that if the *function* of the state in a determinate social formation and the *interests* of the dominant class in this formation *coincide,* it is by reason of the system itself: the direct participation of members of the ruling class in the state apparatus is not the *cause* but the *effect,* and moreover a chance and contingent one, of this objective coincidence.[13]

In this formulation, the functions of the state are broadly determined by the structural imperatives of the capitalist mode of production and the constraints placed on it by the structural environment in which the state must operate. Given these parameters of operation, the state obtains relative autonomy from the various fractions of the capitalist class in order to carry out its functions as a capitalist state. Thus Poulantzas accepts the control of the state by the capitalist class through direct or indirect means or both, but assigns to it relative autonomy vis-à-vis any one *fraction* of that class.[14] Hence, in this formulation, the capitalist state is the state of the capitalist class and serves the interests of that class as a whole; and at the same time it maintains relative autonomy from its various fractions.

Convergence of the Two Views

Miliband, defending himself against vulgar instrumentalist interpretations of his argument, later concedes that the state can and must have a certain degree of autonomy from the capitalist class. Referring to Marx and Engels's assertion that "the modern state is but a committee for managing the common affairs of the whole bourgeoisie," Miliband writes:

This has regularly been taken to mean not only that the state acts *on behalf* of the dominant class . . . but that it acts *at the behest* of that class which is an altogether different assertion and, as I would argue, a vulgar deformation of the thought of Marx and Engels. . . . [T]he notion of common affairs assumes the existence of particular ones; and the notion of the whole bourgeoisie implies the existence of separate elements which make up that whole. This being the case, there is an obvious need for an institution of the kind they refer to, namely the state; and the state *cannot* meet this need without enjoying a certain degree of autonomy. In other words, the notion of autonomy is embedded in the definition itself, is an intrinsic part of it.[15]

Elsewhere, Miliband addresses this question more directly: "Different forms of state have different degrees of autonomy. But all states enjoy some autonomy or independence from all classes, including the dominant classes."[16] Nevertheless,

the relative independence of the state does not reduce its class character: on the contrary, its relative independence makes it *possible* for the state to play its class role in an appropriately flexible manner. If it really was the simple "instrument" of the "ruling class," it would be fatally inhibited in the performance of its role.[17]

He goes on to argue that:

the intervention of the state is always and necessarily partisan: as a class state, it always intervenes for the purpose of maintaining the existing system of domination, even where it intervenes to mitigate the harshness of that system of domination.[18]

Thus Miliband takes a big step toward reconciliation with the relative autonomy thesis while retaining the core of his argument in seeing the capitalist state as an institution controlled by the capitalist class as a whole.

Poulantzas, in his later writings, also moves in a direction away from his earlier position on relative autonomy. He admits that in the current monopoly stage of capitalism, the *monopoly fraction* of the capitalist class dominates the state and thereby secures favorable policies in its own favor over other fractions of the bourgeois power bloc.[19] This situation, he adds, poses problems to the state's traditional role as "political organizer of the general interest of the bourgeoisie" and "restrict[s] the limits of the relative autonomy of the state in relation to monopoly capital and to the field of the compromises it makes with other fractions of the bourgeoisie."[20] The political crisis resulting from this fractional domination and fragmentation, argues Poulantzas, leads to a crisis of the bourgeois state.[21]

Conclusion

With these later reformulations of state theory by both Poulantzas and Miliband, we see a convergence of the two positions and arrive at the general conclusion that the state in capitalist society is both controlled by and, simultaneously, relatively autonomous of the various fractions of the capitalist class, in order to (1) perform its functions in advancing the interests of the capitalist class as a whole, and at the same time (2) maintain its legitimacy over society. This "relative autonomy," however, is rapidly being undermined by the hegemonic (monopoly) fraction of the capitalist class, which as a result is blocking the state's effectiveness in fulfilling its political role as the "executive committee" of the entire bourgeoisie.

More recently, some neo-Weberian theorists have introduced an alternative, "state-centered" approach that grants greater (not less) autonomy to the state and views state managers as autonomous agents who are independent of the prevailing class structure in society. We provide a critical analysis of this approach in the next chapter.

Notes

[1] See Louis Althusser, *For Marx* (London: Penguin, 1969); and idem, *Lenin and Philosophy and Other Essays* (New York: Monthly Review Press, 1971). See also

Louis Althusser and Etienne Balibar, *Reading Capital* (London: New Left Books, 1970).

[2] Althusser, *Lenin and Philosophy and Other Essays*, 135.

[3] Ibid., 137.

[4] Ibid., 185.

[5] Nicos Poulantzas, *Political Power and Social Classes* (London: New Left Books, 1974), 209.

[6] Ibid.

[7] The debate began with a review of Ralph Miliband's *The State in Capitalist Society* (London: Basic Books, 1969) by Nicos Poulantzas, "The Problem of the Capitalist State," *New Left Review*, no. 58 (1969), to which Miliband responded in the next issue of the same journal. See Ralph Miliband, "The Capitalist State—Reply to Nicos Poulantzas," *New Left Review*, no. 59 (1970). See also Nicos Poulantzas, *Political Power and Social Classes* (London: New Left Books, 1974); Ralph Miliband, "Poulantzas and the Capitalist State," *New Left Review*, no. 82 (1973); and Nicos Poulantzas, "The Capitalist State: A Reply to Miliband and Laclau," *New Left Review*, no. 95 (1976). Among Poluantzas's later works, see *Classes in Contemporary Capitalism* (London: New Left Books, 1975) and *State, Power, Socialism* (London: New Left Books, 1978). Miliband's subsequent arguments can be found in his "Political Forms and Historical Materialism," in *Socialist Register*, ed. R. Miliband and J. Saville (London: Merlin Press, 1975) and *Marxism and Politics* (London: Oxford University Press, 1977).

[8] See David Gold, Clarence Y.H. Lo, and Erik Olin Wright, "Some Recent Developments in Marxist Theories of the Capitalist State," pts. 1 and 2, *Monthly Review* (October and November 1975); Gosta Esping-Andersen, Roger Friedland, and Erik Olin Wright, "Modes of Class Struggle and the Capitalist State," *Kapitalistate*, nos. 4–5 (Summer 1976); Albert Szymanski, *The Capitalist State and the Politics of Class* (Cambridge, Mass.: Winthrop, 1978); Bob Jessop, *The Capitalist State* (New York: New York University Press, 1982); Martin Carnoy, *The State and Political Theory* (Princeton: Princeton University Press, 1984).

[9] Miliband, *The State in Capitalist Society*, 23.

[10] Gold, Lo, and Wright, "Marxist Theories of the Capitalist State," 33.

[11] Ibid., 32–33.

[12] Poulantzas, "Problem of the Capitalist State," 73.

[13] Ibid.

[14] Poulantzas, *Political Power*; and idem, *State, Power, Socialism*.

[15] Miliband, "Poulantzas and the Capitalist State," 85.

[16] Miliband, *Marxism and Politics*, 83.

[17] Ibid., 87.

[18] Ibid., 91.

[19] Nicos Poulantzas, "The Political Crisis and the Crisis of the State," in *Critical Sociology: European Perspectives*, ed. J.W. Freiberg (New York: Irvington, 1979), 374–81.

[20] Ibid., 375.

[21] Ibid., 357–93.

13   TRIMBERGER, BLOCK, AND SKOCPOL AND NEO-WEBERIAN THEORIZING

This chapter examines a number of contemporary attempts in neo-Weberian theorizing on the state and society by theorists influenced by the Weberian school—Ellen Kay Trimberger, Fred Block, and Theda Skocpol. Providing a political theory of state-society relations, these theorists stress the autonomy of the state vis-à-vis the dominant and dominated classes and characterize the state as a source of power independent of the contending class forces.[1]

In what follows we present a critical analysis of the main arguments advanced by these theorists and contrast their views to the Marxist theory of the state discussed in the previous chapter.

Autonomous Bureaucrats and Political Power

Ellen Kay Trimberger, in her book *Revolution from Above*, attempts to develop a neo-Weberian theory of the state and society, arguing that the state should be seen as playing an independent role and state bureaucrats as independent agents free of class control. "A bureaucratic state apparatus, or a segment of it can be said to be relatively autonomous," Trimberger writes, "when those who hold high civil and/or military posts satisfy two conditions":

> (1) They are not recruited from the dominant landed, commercial or industrial classes; and (2) they do not form close personal and economic ties with these classes after their elevation to high office. Relatively autonomous bureaucrats are thus independent of those classes which control the means of production.[2]

Trimberger goes on to argue that "dynamically autonomous bureaucrats enter the class struggle as an *independent* force, rather than as an instrument of other class forces."[3] Going a step further, she contends that these bureaucrats "have a distinctive class position" and that they can "use their control over state resources—coercive, monetary, and ideological—to destroy the existing economic and class order."[4] Moreover:

> even in polities where the state bureaucracy is subordinate to a party and parliamentary system controlled by [dominant] class interests . . . , relatively autonomous military officers have the potential for breaking this institutional subordination by force.[5]

If, as Trimberger contends, these "autonomous" bureaucrats hold on to no particular class interests of their own (or those of other classes), it is not clear why they would be "acting to destroy an existing economic and class order" in crisis situations.[6] What Trimberger fails to tell us is (1) the class ideology of these bureaucrats (which is substantially, but not exclusively, determined by their class origin); (2) the class interests they intend to serve (which is related to the above considerations of origin, ideology, or both), and, most important, (3) the structural consequences of policies pursued by these bureaucrats and their positive or negative impact on different classes.

Trimberger's general contention that "control of the governing apparatus is a source of power independent of that held by class"[7] constitutes a departure from the Marxist theory of the state discussed in the previous chapter. She confirms this departure by stating that

> neither the Marxist nor the non-Marxist political sociology of Third World societies has looked at the relationship between the state apparatus and dominant classes as an *independent* variable determining the type and rate of change in the transition from agrarian to industrial societies.[8]

In this sense, the approach taken by Trimberger on this issue is in effect a restatement of a revised version of the Weberian position.

State Managers and Power Politics

An extension of this line of reasoning has led other theorists in a pluralist direction where, as evidenced in Fred Block's argument, the state and state officials become "autonomous agents," so that they acquire independence from the capitalist class and, further, determine policy over the heads of this class, including the formulation of policies that sometimes go *against* the interests of the capitalists as a whole.[9]

In his controversial article "The Ruling Class Does Not Rule," Block attacks the structuralist position of Poulantzas as "a slightly more sophisticated version" of instrumentalism and proposes to replace it with his own reformulation of the problem. The underlying argument advanced by Block against the structuralist-instrumentalist problematic discussed in the previous chapter rests on his conception of the role of "state managers," who, according to Block, are autonomous agents functioning in their own self (or positional) interests and are not consciously engaged in the protection of the interests of the capitalist class as such. Thus, Block introduces into the debate "autonomous state managers" controlled by no one and subservient to no particular class interests other than their own—although they are forced to formulate policies within the framework of an environment that includes both capitalist domination of the economy and class struggle between the two contending class forces, the capitalists and the workers. This becomes clear when Block states: "State managers do have an interest in expanding their own power, including their own power to manage the economy."[10] To back up this claim, Block writes: "German capitalists were reduced to being functionaries, albeit highly paid functionaries, of the Nazi state that was acting in its own profoundly irrational interests."[11]

Elsewhere, Block asserts that "the rationality of the capitalist state emerges out of the three-sided relationship between state managers, capital and subordinate classes."[12] Referring to his own theoretical formulation, and distancing himself from Marxism, he writes:

The virtue of this model is that it allows one to get away from the standard Marxist methodological tool of as-

suming that state policies always reflect the intention-
ality of a social class or sector of a class. It renders
obsolete the procedure of looking for a specific social
base for any particular state policy.[13]

He goes on to assert:

One can say that a policy objectively benefited a particular social class, but that is very different from saying
that this social class, or sector of a class, subjectively
wanted the policy or that its intentions were a critical
element in policy development.[14]

This leads him to conclude: "The road to analytic confusion in
Marxism is paved with an exaggerated concern with class intention-
ality."[15]

Block's critique of Marxism, for its "narrow focus on 'class
struggles,'" has during the past decade taken him down what he calls
a "Post-Marxist" path, rejecting historical materialism altogether. In
his recent book *Revising State Theory* Block continues to see the
state as an autonomous agent, arguing that politics is "irreducible"
and that social struggles, such as those around race and gender,
cannot be explained as manifestations of class struggle.[16] Advocating
a position that would "go beyond Marxism," Block asserts: "The
answers that Marx offered no longer suffice, and just as Marx sought
to transcend Hegel, so too, those who pursue the Post-Marxist
project seek to transcend Marx."[17] This, he feels, would free him to
introduce into his analysis

many other collective actors organized around race,
gender, age, sexual orientation, religious orientation, or
shared views about the environment or the arms race. In
place of a narrow focus on "class struggles," the emphasis
would be on a broad range of social struggles.[18]

Block's seemingly "broader" reformulation of state theory,
which allows state managers considerable autonomy while bringing
in a multitude of social actors beyond classes, unfortunately turns
out to be a "slightly more sophisticated version" of recent neo-

Weberian approaches than a new attempt at a reconstruction of prevailing Marxist theories of the state and society.

Class, State, and Society: A "State-Centered" Approach

Other neo-Weberian theorists, like Theda Skocpol, have adopted an approach similar to that of Trimberger and Block in conceptualizing the state as an independent force, and in the process have come to embrace a more elaborate "state-centered" approach, rejecting the Marxist position on the class nature of the state.[19] Influenced by Weberian theory, Skocpol in her book *States and Social Revolutions* attempts to counter the classical Marxist position on the relationship of the state to the mode of production and the class basis of politics and the state.[20] She writes:

> In contrast to most (especially recent) Marxist theories, this view refuses to treat states as if they were mere analytic aspects of abstractly conceived modes of production, or even political aspects of concrete class relations and struggles. Rather it insists that states are actual organizations controlling (or attempting to control) territories and people.[21]

Arguing in favor of the view that the state is an entity with "an autonomous structure—a structure with a logic and interests of its own,"[22] Skocpol examines the French, Russian, and Chinese revolutions in terms of the centrality of the state's role in "acting for itself." Adopting an "organizational" and "realist" perspective on the state,[23] "state and party organizations," she argues, must be viewed "as *independent* determinants of political conflicts and outcomes."[24] Thus, for Skocpol "the state organizations . . . have a more central and autonomous place" because, like Trimberger and Block, she sees in the state "potential autonomy of action over . . . the dominant class and existing relations of production."[25]

In this reformulation of the class-state problematic, the state is divorced from and opposed to existing social classes and acts in accordance with its distinct interests, based primarily on the maintenance of internal order and competition against external forces (i.e., other states) threatening its survival.

> The state normally performs two basic sets of tasks: It maintains order, and it competes with other actual or potential states. . . . [T]he state's own fundamental interest in maintaining sheer physical order and political peace may lead it—especially in periods of crisis—to enforce concessions to subordinate-class demands. These concessions may be at the expense of the interests of the dominant class, but not contrary to the state's own interests in controlling the population and collecting taxes and military recruits.[26]

Thus:

> If state organizations cope with whatever tasks they already claim smoothly and efficiently, legitimacy . . . will probably be accorded to the state's form and rulers by most groups in society. . . . Loss of legitimacy, especially among the crucial [politically powerful] groups, tends to ensue with a vengeance if and when . . . the state fails consistently to cope with existing tasks, or proves unable to cope with new tasks suddenly thrust upon it by crisis circumstances.[27]

"The political crises that have launched social revolutions," writes Skocpol, "have not at all been epiphenomenal reflections of societal strains or class contradictions. Rather, they have been direct expressions of contradictions centered in the structures of old-regime states."[28] Thus, to understand better those processes by which the state has taken center stage of history, Skocpol suggests "the need for a more state-centered approach" in studying states and social revolutions.[29]

Some Concluding Observations

Contrary to the Trimberger, Block, and Skocpol formulations, one could argue that although the state can, and sometimes does, gain limited autonomy from the direct control of main class forces in society (especially during periods of crises), this autonomy by no means implies the class neutrality of the state and its agents, that the state and state officials are "above class."

Clearly, the state cannot be seen in terms distinct from class forces and class struggles in society. However independent it may at times *appear* to be, the state, as the supreme superstructural institution in society, is in the final analysis a reflection of the underlying mode of production defined by definite relations of production that characterize the class nature of that state.

This understanding of the materialist dynamics of history lies at the heart of Marx's class analysis which we discussed at the beginning of this book. In the final, closing pages of this book we return to this theme once again, where Goran Therborn and Albert Szymanski make the point that it is only through such an analytical approach that a more complete understanding of the relationship between the state and society can be obtained, and the real nature of politics and the state revealed.

Before turning to historical materialism and class analysis, however, we take up in the next chapter another important contemporary theory that developed a significant following during the past two decades—that of "world systems theory."

Notes

[1] See E.K. Trimberger, *Revolution from Above: Military Bureaucrats and Development in Japan, Turkey, and Peru* (New Brunswick, N.J.: Transaction Books, 1978); Theda Skocpol, *States and Revolutions: A Comparative Analysis of France, Russia and China* (Cambridge, England: Cambridge University Press, 1979); Fred Block, "The Ruling Class Does Not Rule: Notes on the Marxist Theory of the State," *Socialist Review*, no. 33 (May–June 1977).

[2] Trimberger, *Revolution from Above*, 4.

[3] Ibid., 5; emphasis added.

[4] Ibid., 4.

[5] Ibid.

[6] Ibid., 4–5.

[7] Ibid., 7.

[8] Ibid., 8.

[9] See Block, "The Ruling Class Does Not Rule"; and idem, "Class Consciousness and Capitalist Rationalization: A Reply to Critics," *Socialist Review*, nos. 40–41 (July–October 1978).

[10] Ibid., 40–41.

[11] Ibid., 219.

[12] Fred Block, "Marxist Theories of the State in World System Analysis," paper presented at the First Annual Political Economy of the World System Conference, American University, Washington, D.C., March–April 1977, 8.

[13] Ibid.

[14] Ibid.

[15] Ibid.

[16] Fred Block, *Revising State Theory* (Philadelphia: Temple University Press, 1987), 17–18, 34–35.

[17] Ibid., 35.

[18] Ibid., 18.

[19] In acknowledging the affinity of his approach to state theory to Skocpol's "state-centered" approach, which we discuss later in the chapter, Block writes: "The systematization of a state-centered approach in the work of Theda Skocpol has been the other important new development in state theory. Skocpol has energetically argued that both the liberal and the Marxist traditions have been society-centered, explaining what goes on in the state as a function of what goes on in society. Her alternative is a state-centered approach that would provide a corrective to the standard view by stressing the diverse ways in which the state structures social life." Ibid., 20.

[20] Skocpol, *States and Social Revolutions.* For an acknowledgment of this and other influences on Skocpol's views, see ibid., 301, notes 73 and 77.

[21] Ibid., 31.

[22] Ibid., 27. In developing this view of the state, Skocpol cites the works of Trimberger and Block, among others, and states: "I have been very greatly influenced by these writings, and by personal conversations with Trimberger and Block." Ibid., 301, note 73.

[23] Ibid., 31.

[24] Theda Skocpol, "Political Response to Capitalist Crisis: Neo-Marxist Theories of the State and the Case of the New Deal," *Politics and Society* 10, no. 2 (1981): 199.

[25] Skocpol, *States and Social Revolutions*, 31.

[26] Ibid., 30.

[27] Ibid., 31–32.

[28] Ibid., 29.

[29] Ibid.

14 WALLERSTEIN AND
WORLD SYSTEMS THEORY

Over the past two decades, since the publication in 1974 of his *The Modern World-System*, Immanuel Wallerstein has played a central role in the formulation of a theory of the global political economy that came to be known as "world systems theory."[1] Providing a comparative-historical approach to the study of societies across national boundaries, Wallerstein has thus introduced a unique perspective to social analysis of states at the global level.

This chapter focuses on the arguments presented by Wallerstein in favor of his world systems perspective, which has become prominent among a group of social scientists who developed an entire school of thought around this theory.

World Systems Theory

With the publication in the mid-1970s of *The Modern World-System*, Wallerstein launched a multivolume study of the origins and development of the modern world system in an effort to reexamine the transition from feudalism to capitalism in western Europe and its subsequent development and expansion to the rest of the world.[2] This was followed by Samir Amin's two-volume study of accumulation on a world scale and other studies of the world accumulation process from earlier times to the present.[3] Thus began the formation of an entire school of thought that eventually came to be known as "world systems theory."[4]

Explaining his method in selecting the world system as the unit of analysis, Wallerstein argues that he

> abandoned the idea altogether of taking either the sovereign state or that vaguer concept, the national society, as the unit of analysis. I decided that neither one was a social system and that one could only speak of social

127

change in social systems. The only social system in this scheme was the world system.[5]

"Once we assume that the unit of analysis is such a world-system and not the state or the nation or the people," Wallerstein argues, "then much changes in the outcome of the analysis."

> Most specifically we shift from a concern with the attributive characteristics of states to concern with the relational characteristics of states. We shift from seeing classes (and status groups) as groups within a state to seeing them as groups within a world-economy.[6]

Conceptualizing global power struggles as those in accordance with the requirements of a world system that dominates the global political economy over an entire historical period, the world systems approach attempts to provide tools of analysis to examine contemporary global political developments in the context of the logic of the capitalist world economy that has come to dominate the structure of economic relations on a world scale since the sixteenth century.

The capitalist world economy, argues Wallerstein, brings capitalist and noncapitalist states alike under its sway and determines the nature and course of their development as dictated by the most powerful state in control of the world system in a given historical epoch. But competition and rivalry between the leading states engaged in the struggle for domination of the world system, leaves open the possibility that a dominant state in a particular historical period will be replaced by another:

> While the advantages of the core-states have not ceased to expand throughout the history of the modern world-system, the ability of a particular state to remain in the core sector is not beyond challenge. The hounds are ever to the hares for the position of top dog. Indeed, it may well be that in this kind of system it is not structurally possible to avoid, over a long period of historical time, a circulation of elites in the sense that the particular country that is dominant at a given time tends to be replaced in this role sooner or later by another country.[7]

Moving beyond nation-states and formulating the problem in world-systemic terms, Wallerstein thus provides an alternative explanation of the rise and fall of world systems, which take place in much longer historical periods and constitute the very basis of world historical transformations.

In "The Rise and Future Demise of the World Capitalist System," Wallerstein argues in favor of just such a conceptualization in explaining the origins, development, and future transformation of the capitalist world economy and system.[8] Likewise, situating the problematic in a broader historical context of systemic transformation, Wallerstein elsewhere, in *The Modern World-System* and later in *The Capitalist World-Economy*, attempts to explain the transition from feudalism to capitalism in Western Europe and the subsequent rise and development of the world capitalist system in such world-systemic terms.[9]

The Three-Tiered Model

An essential element in the global analysis of the modern world system is the theory's three-tiered model of "core," "periphery," and "semiperiphery," which divides the world system into three areas or zones defined on the basis of a society's level of development and incorporation into the world system. Moreover, the political-economic content of such incorporation determines whether a given social formation is part of the core, the periphery, or the semi-periphery.[10]

> The organizing principle of this operation is the categorical differentiation of levels of the world-system: core, semiperiphery, and periphery. These zones, distinguished by their different economic functions within the world-economic division of labor . . . structure the assemblage of productive processes that constitute the capitalist world-economy.[11]

"On a world-scale," write Hopkins and Wallerstein, "the processes of the division of labor that define and integrate the world-economy are . . . [those] which we designate as 'core' and 'periphery.'"[12] Moreover, "although obviously derivative from the core-periphery conception," they add, "there exists a third category, structurally distinct from core and periphery": "Looking at the world-economy as a whole, . . . [there exists] a basically triadic world-scale division of labor among, now, core states, semiperipheral states, and peripheral areas."[13] Thus:

> The world-economy became basically structured as an increasingly interrelated system of strong "core" and weak "peripheral" states, in which inter-state relations . . . are continually shaped and in turn continually shape the deepening and expanding world-scale division and integration of production.[14]

This brings up the question of "the network(s) of governance or rule in the area in question."[15] "In this respect," write Hopkins and Wallerstein, "incorporation entails the expansion of the world-economy's interstate system":

> Interstate relations and the interstate system overall, in part express and in part circumscribe or structure the world-scale accumulation/production process. In short, the relational networks forming the interstate system are integral to, not outside of, the networks constitutive of the social economy defining the scope and reach of the modern world-system. . . .
>
> Insofar as external areas are incorporated, then— and in the singular development of the modern world-system all have been—the transition period framing incorporation encloses definite directions of change in a once external area's arrangements and processes of rule or governance.[16]

The main feature of the modern world system is, in essence, the transfer of surplus from the periphery to the core of the system, conceptualized in a manner similar to Andre Gunder Frank's "metropolis-satellite" model of domination and "exploitation."[17] The mechanism whereby this transfer takes place is "unequal exchange"[18]—a mechanism made possible by the domination of peripheral states by those in the core:

Once we get a difference in the strength of the state machineries, we get the operation of "unequal exchange" which is enforced by strong states on weak ones, by core states on peripheral areas. Thus capitalism involves not only appropriation of the surplus value by an owner from a laborer, but an appropriation of surplus of the whole-world-economy by core areas. And this was as true in the stage of agricultural capitalism as it is in the stage of industrial capitalism.[19]

More specifically, Wallerstein argues that without this process of unequal exchange, the capitalist world economy could not exist:

> Such a system [of unequal exchange] is *necessary* for the expansion of a world market if the primary consideration is *profit*. Without *unequal* exchange, it would not be *profitable* to expand the size of the division of labor. And without such expansion, it would not be profitable to maintain a capitalist world-economy, which would then either disintegrate or revert to the form of a redistributive world-empire.[20]

Despite the subordination of peripheral states to those in the core, and the "exploitation" of the former by the latter through surplus extraction, the modern world system allows, under certain conditions and in the context of certain political-economic processes, the transformation of some peripheral states into semiperipheral ones. But such transformation (or mobility) of states along the three-tiered continuum takes place within the context and logic of the system as a whole and as a consequence of the dictates of the dominant world system in a given historical period. Thus the various parts of the system that make up its totality always function within the framework of the relationship of the parts to the whole.

Conclusion

Although world systems theory constitutes a major improvement over mainstream developmentalist theories of the world political economy, it nevertheless suffers from a number of fundamental flaws that must be pointed out. The first, and central, flaw of this theory is the treatment of the world economy and the world system in strictly circulationist terms. Capitalism, defined as a system of accumulation for profit through the market, is conceptualized in the context of exchange relations. Thus, economic relations take place between states within the context of such market exchange. As a result, the question of the mode of production, and its social component relations of production (i.e., class relations), are ignored or eliminated from analysis so that class struggles based on relations of production also disappear from analysis as irrelevant. We are thus left with the generalized abstract notions of "world system" and "world economy" consisting of three zones ("core," "periphery," and "semiperiphery") between which all major global social, political, and economic relations take place. Unfortunately, given its focus on the world system at the global level, the theory fails to provide an explanation of the underlying *class logic* of the world system, its class contradictions and class conflicts.

In the next chapter, we turn to the Marxist class analysis approach provided in the works of Goran Therborn and Albert Szymanski, who introduce into contemporary social theory recent developments in Marxist theory.

Notes

[1] Immanuel Wallerstein, *The Modern World-System* (New York: Academic Press, 1974), 53.

[2] Ibid.

[3] Samir Amin, *Accumulation on a World Scale*, 2 vols. (New York: Monthly Review Press, 1974); Richard Rubinson, ed., *Dynamics of World Development* (London: Sage Publications, 1981). See also the works of Terence Hopkins, Christopher Chase-Dunn, Albert Bergesen, Walter Goldfrank, and Terry Boswell.

[4] For an in-depth analysis of the theoretical and methodological premises of world systems theory, see Alvin Y. So, *Social Change and Development: Modernization, Dependency, and World-System Theories* (Newbury Park, Calif.: Sage Publications, 1990), pt. 3.

[5] Wallerstein, *The Modern World-System*, 7.

[6] Ibid., xi.

[7] Immanuel Wallerstein, "The Rise and Future Demise of the World Capitalist System," *Comparative Studies in Society and History* 16 (September 1974): 350.

[8] Ibid.

[9] See Wallerstein, *The Modern World-System*; and idem, *The Capitalist World-Economy* (Cambridge, England: Cambridge University Press, 1979).

[10] Wallerstein, *The Modern World-System*; and idem, "The Rise and Future Demise of the World Capitalist System."

[11] Terence K. Hopkins and Immanuel Wallerstein, *World-Systems Analysis* (Beverly Hills, Calif.: Sage Publications, 1982), 77.

[12] Ibid., 45.

[13] Ibid., 47.

[14] Ibid., 43.

[15] Terence K. Hopkins and Immanuel Wallerstein, "Structural Transformations of the World-Economy," in Rubinson, *Dynamics of World Development*, 245.

[16] Ibid., 245–46.

[17] See Andre Gunder Frank, *Capitalism and Underdevelopment in Latin America* (New York: Monthly Review Press, 1967).

[18] This process was first examined at length by Arghiri Emmanuel, *Unequal Exchange: A Study of the Imperialism of Trade* (New York: Monthly Review Press, 1972). Later it was elaborated by Samir Amin, *Unequal Development: An Essay on the Social Formations of Peripheral Capitalism* (New York: Monthly Review Press, 1977).

[19] Wallerstein, *The Capitalist World-Economy*, 18–19.

[20] Ibid., 71.

15

THERBORN AND SZYMANSKI ON CONTEMPORARY MARXIST THEORY

In contrast to the neo-Weberian and world systems theories discussed in the previous two chapters, we now present an overview of recent developments in Marxist theory by focusing on the works of Goran Therborn and Albert Szymanski who provide an alternative, historical-materialist conceptualization of class, state, and society.[1] Advancing a class-based position and incorporating some of the important Marxist theorizing of the 1970s and 1980s into a social theory based on a class-analysis approach informed by the dialectics of the class struggle, Therborn and Szymanski make an important contribution to the resurgence of Marxist theory in recent years.

Historical Materialism and the Base-Superstructure Problematic

The origins of this new wave of Marxist theorizing go back to the late 1970s, when Therborn, Szymanski, and a number of other Marxist intellectuals set forth their theoretical position and thus prepared the stage for the subsequent emergence of works raising questions of paramount importance originally formulated by Marx, Engels, and Lenin.

"This renaissance of Marxist political analysis in the 1980's," writes Therborn, "will appear unexpected":

> The irony is that while many former protagonists and
> adherents of various "schools" of neo-Marxism are now
> proclaiming a post-Marxist, beyond-class stance, a new,
> vigorous self-confident class theory of politics and the
> state is being launched, impeccably dressed in the best
> clothes of modern empirical social science, while mak-

ing no secret of its inspiring commitment to the working-class movement. . . .
There is, then, still a contingent of scholars arguing
that states are a function of classes, rather than the other
way round.[2]

To his credit, Therborn's contribution to this renaissance has led to
a flood of studies in Marxist political economy and class theory of
the state and society in the 1980s.

In his book *What Does the Ruling Class Do When It Rules?*
Therborn argues in favor of the historical-materialist approach to the
study of society, the state, and politics. The aim of such approach,
he writes, "is to show that different types of class relations and of
class power generate corresponding forms of state organization, and
to elucidate the way in which the class character of the state
apparatus is determined and revealed."[3]

According to the axioms of historical materialism, class
and state condition each other: where there are no
classes, there is no state. In class societies, moreover,
social relations are first and foremost class relations.
Thus, by definition, every state has a class character,
and every class society has a ruling class (or bloc of
ruling classes).[4]

Contrary to Hegelian-Marxist and neo-Weberian notions of
"state autonomy" and "state-centered" theories that assign primacy
to the state and superstructural institutions in society, Therborn
reintroduces into the debate the "base-superstructure" problematic,
interpreted in a new light—one that avoids economistic
conceptualizations of politics on the one hand, while rejecting
eclectic "codeterminist" notions of class and state on the other.
Basic to Therborn's analysis of the relationship of the economic
base to the political superstructure is the role of the *class struggle*
engendered by the dominant mode of production. "In very general
terms," writes Therborn,

the character of state power is defined by the two
fundamental processes of determination of the super-

structure by the base—processes which in reality are
two aspects of the same determination. One of these is
the systemic logic of social modes of production, that is
to say, the tendencies and contradictions of the specific
dynamic of each mode. The other is the struggle of
classes, defined by their position in the mode of production. These two forms of determination by the base
are logically interrelated in the basic theory of historical
materialism.[5]

In this formulation, the state is no longer viewed simply as a
passive recipient of directives from the dominant class but is
actively involved in the reproduction of the dominant relations of
production: "Invariably the state enters into the reproduction of the
relations of production by providing the latter with a stabilizing legal
framework backed by force."[6] Moreover, the relations of production, Therborn points out, are structured by legal boundaries which
define relations between dominant and subordinate classes.[7]

To sum up Therborn's position, "the economic base determines
the political superstructure by entering into the reproduction of state
power and the state apparatus" and "shapes the character of state
power by, among other things, providing the basic parameters of
state action."[8] Further, because "exploitative relations of production
need a repressive political apparatus as their ultimate guarantee,"[9]
the state comes to assume this role to "promote and defend the ruling
class and its mode of exploitation or supremacy."[10] Thus, "the ruling
class exercises its ruling power over other classes and strata through
the state—through holding state power."[11] In order to maintain its
legitemacy and secure social order, however, "the state must *mediate*
the exploitation or domination of the ruling class over other classes
and strata."[12]

Viewing the base-superstructure problematic in these terms,
Therborn bridges the gap between structuralist and instrumentalist
formulations of the state and provides a dialectical analysis of the
relationship between class and state, thus advancing the debate
through a fresh look at historical materialism as the basis for a
resurgent Marxist theory of society in this final decade of the
twentieth century.

Theory of the State

Albert Szymanski, in his book *The Capitalist State and the Politics of Class*, makes a similar case in favor of the historical-materialist approach to the study of society and the state.[13] Citing the works of Marx, Engels, and Lenin on the state, Szymanski argues that the state plays a central role in society and that "a Marxist political sociology must thus give careful and detailed consideration to the nature of the state."[14]

Examining the nature and role of the state in class society in general and capitalist society in particular, Szymanski writes:

> The state is an instrument by which the exploitation of the economically subordinate class is secured by the economically dominant class that controls the state. . . . The social relationships and the social order that the state guarantees are thus the social relationships of inequality and the order of property and exploitation. . . .
>
> The state in capitalist society is a capitalist state by virtue of its domination by the capitalist class *and* in that it functions most immediately in the interests of capital.[15]

Moreover, the state must function within the confines of an economic, military, political, and ideological environment structured by capitalist relations of production.[16] This means that the logic of capitalist economic relations, reinforced by capital's ideological hegemony, dictate the policies the state must follow, which are formulated within a very limited range of options allowed by the capitalist mode of production. Thus the state in capitalist society is controlled by the capitalist class through both direct and indirect mechanisms that foster the interests of this class.

Far from providing a simple instrumentalist view of the state, Szymanski reveals the full range and complexity of the state's actions in response to the ensuing class struggles in society: "Political outcomes are the result of the relative size, social location, consciousness, degree of organization, and strategies followed by classes and segments of classes in their ongoing struggles."[17] He goes on to point out that "no one class or segment of a class is ever able totally to control all aspects of society."[18] Moreover, while the state "is normally under the domination of the class that owns and controls the means of production,"

> the ruling class must take into account both the demands and likely responses of other classes when it makes state policy. If it does not it may suffer very serious consequences, including social revolution.[19]

"The degree of relative autonomy of the state bureaucracy from direct capitalist-class domination," writes Szymanski, "can either decrease *or* increase drastically during an economic and social crisis":

> A state that is too directly dominated by the majority bloc of the capitalist class may be unable to handle such a crisis, because the narrow-minded self-interest of this bloc prevents the state it dominates from adopting the policies necessary to save and advance the system. Domination of the state by these groups also tends to discredit the state, which because of such control is obviously not alleviating an economic crisis. The legitimating function of the state thus comes into increasing conflict with direct capitalist-class control.[20]

Providing an empirical path out of the structuralist-instrumentalist problematic, Szymanski argues that some states are dominated principally by direct mechanisms, while others are dominated by indirect mechanisms, and still others are dominated by *both*.

Commenting on the question of relative autonomy, David Gold, Clarence Y.H. Lo, and Erik Olin Wright make a similar argument when they point out that such autonomy "is not an invariant feature of the capitalist state":

> Particular capitalist states will be more or less autonomous depending upon the degree of internal divisiveness, the contradictions within the various classes and fractions which constitute the power bloc, and upon the

intensity of class struggle between the working class
and the capitalist class as a whole.[21]

In Europe, for example, given the differential political development of some European formations (e.g., France, Italy, Spain, and
Greece) where strong socialist and communist parties and movements
have developed and flourished, it has been difficult for capital to
maintain direct, exclusive control of the state apparatus and yield
results always in line with its interests. In these formations, the state
has been shaped not only by the various fractions of the capitalist
class but also by the representatives of rival opposition forces,
including the socialists and the communists, contending for state
power. This situation has invariably been effected through the
presence of opposition forces within the very organs and institutions
of the state. As the power and influence of these parties have
increased disproportionately vis-à-vis that of the capitalists, a resurgence of the class struggle and struggles for state power have
occurred—sometimes leading to the possession of political power
by socialist and communist forces in key state institutions, such as
the parliament or the presidency and cabinet posts within the
executive branch, as in Spain, France, Italy, and Greece, as well as
elsewhere in Europe at various levels of government in local and
national politics.

In contrast, in the United States, except possibly during crisis
periods (such as the Great Depression of the 1930s) when there has
been a resurgence of class politics, the state has been completely
dominated and controlled by the capitalist class, now especially by
its monopoly fraction. This, coupled with the relative weakness of
the U.S. labor movement, has led capital to directly control the U.S.
state. Thus, it is not surprising that an instrumentalist view of the
state has so readily become the predominant mode of state theorizing
among Marxists in the United States.

The greater strength and militancy of the organized working-
class movement and effective opposition of independent workers'
parties and organizations in Europe, on the other hand, has effected
the distribution of power among a multitude of political parties and
coalition governments. Thus, it is likewise not surprising that a
structuralist theory of the state would emerge to provide an alternative

explanation of the nature and dynamics of politics and the state in Europe during this same period.

Thus the role of direct and indirect mechanisms of capitalist-class rule, as well as the degree of autonomy of the state, has varied considerably among formations dominated by the capitalist mode of production. These variations point to the need for a concrete analysis of states across national boundaries and over extended historical periods.

Conclusion

The centerpiece of the resurgent Marxist theory of society and the state has been its focus on the nature of class relations, class struggles, and the class character of the state. Situated within the framework of the base-superstructure problematic of historical materialism, Marxist theory has taken center stage in social theorizing and is now experiencing a resurgence among a growing contingent of critical social theorists in addressing the pressing problems of contemporary capitalist society. Therborn and Szymanski have been among the pioneers of this resurgence of critical thinking in sociology and the social sciences during the 1980s; others, promoting their views among a new generation of critical social theorists, are now playing a central role in the development of this important trend in social theory in the decade of the 1990s and into the next century.

Notes

[1] For Therborn's most important works, see Goran Therborn, *Science, Class and Society* (London: New Left Books, 1976), esp. 317–429; idem, *What Does the Ruling Class Do When It Rules?* (London: New Left Books, 1978); and idem, *The Ideology of Power and the Power of Ideology* (London: New Left Books, 1980). For some of Szymanski's most important works, see Albert Szymanski, *The Capitalist State and the Politics of Class* (Cambridge, Mass.: Winthrop, 1978); idem, *The Logic of Imperialism* (New York: Praeger, 1981); and idem, *Class Structure: A Critical Perspective* (New York: Praeger, 1983).

[2] Goran Therborn, "Neo-Marxist, Pluralist, Corporatist, Statist Theories and the Welfare State," in *The State in Global Perspective*, ed. A. Kazancigil (Aldershot, England: Gower and UNESCO, 1986), 205–6.

[3] Therborn, *What Does the Ruling Class Do?* 35.

[4] Ibid., 132.

[5] Ibid., 162.

[6] Ibid., 165.

[7] Ibid.

[8] Ibid., 169.

[9] Therborn, *Science, Class and Society*, 400–1.

[10] Therborn, *What Does the Ruling Class Do?*, 181.

[11] Ibid.

[12] Ibid.

[13] Szymanski, *The Capitalist State and the Politics of Class*.

[14] Ibid., 20–21.

[15] Ibid., 21, 25.

[16] Ibid., 24.

[17] Ibid., 27.

[18] Ibid.

[19] Ibid.

[20] Ibid., 273.

[21] David Gold, Clarence Y.H. Lo, and Erik Olin Wright, "Some Recent Developments in Marxist Theories of the Capitalist State," *Monthly Review* 27, nos. 5–6 (October and November, 1975): 38.

Chapter **16** CONCLUSION

The varieties of social theory discussed in this brief introductory book represent a sampling of the rich heritage of diverse theoretical perspectives in sociology and related disciplines in the social sciences. They provide us with a multitude of explanations on different aspects of social life, encompassing the economy, society, and polity. While the traditions of classical social theory inform contemporary theorizing in sociology, thus cultivating the contributions of the great social thinkers of the past century, modern social theorists of the twentieth century have made their own unique contribution to the study of society, providing answers to the burning questions of our time from a variety of diverse theoretical perspectives.

Although Durkheim, Weber, and Marx are viewed as classical reference points in sociological theory, representing the three alternative approaches—organic, individualistic, and organizational—that have come to define the boundaries of the rival schools of thought in contemporary sociology, other, though somewhat less influential, theorists of the late nineteenth and early twentieth centuries have also made important contributions to classical and contemporary social theory, so that theorists as diverse as Pareto, Freud, Gramsci, Du Bois, Parsons, Merton, Mills, Poulantzas, Wallerstein, and Therborn have made their mark within the broader parameters of modern social theory.

This accumulated source of knowledge over the past century, with parallel developments in a variety of competing paradigms in social theory, has led to a combination of diverse approaches yielding numerous new theoretical syntheses (e.g., neo-Weberian, neo-Marxist, and neo-Freudian), as well as the establishment of entire schools of thought cultivated by such intellectual cross-fertilization (e.g., the Frankfurt School of critical theory, structural functionalism, symbolic interactionism, and varieties of structuralist theorizing).

142

More recently, there has emerged "postmodernist" modes of thought, which attempt to explain the contours of the "postcapitalist" social order. Theorists opting for this most recent attempt at critical theorizing, which rejects both mainstream and Marxist analyses of contemporary society, have introduced into their cultural analysis the theory and praxis of "postmodernity," an era that allegedly characterizes contemporary, "postindustrial" society. These self-defined analysts of the "postmodern age," however, have come under strong criticism for promoting yet another fad in social theory whose roots lie in the pessimism prevalent in a period of decline and decay in centers of world capitalism in the closing decades of the twentieth century.

The theoretical defects in postmodernist discourse on the nature and sources of this transformation notwithstanding, the contemporary crisis of world capitalism has generated intense discussion and debate between and within the leading schools of thought and engendered the emergence of a variety of alternative theoretical positions. Clearly, social theory cannot be divorced from the prevailing material conditions in society. And these conditions often give rise to a variety of intellectual responses that evolve into various theoretical positions that, in turn, attempt to address the social transformations we are experiencing today. Thus the dialectical interaction between theory and practice over time comes to inform our conception of the social world and further contributes to a better understanding of the prevailing conditions in society.

We have in this book attempted to provide a glimpse of classical and contemporary attempts by a variety of social theorists to tackle the central questions of our time—questions that define the human condition in all its complexities. Theorists with differing views on human nature, the nature of society, the role of the individual and social institutions, as well as other dimensions of social, economic, and political life that define the totality of social relations and the social order, have made eloquent arguments in favor of their positions on these questions, which we have critically examined in this book.

We have shown that much of the theoretical discourse among the classical social theorists of the late nineteenth and early twentieth centuries has been in reaction to the arguments advanced by Marx on a variety of questions concerning society. Durkheim, Weber,

Pareto, Mosca, Michels, Freud, Gramsci, Lenin, and a host of other social theorists of this period developed their theories as an extension of or in direct opposition to the ideas expounded by Marx, who is viewed by many as the greatest social theorist of the nineteenth century. Through a brilliant transformation of the Hegelian dialectic and a dynamic reconceptualization of classical materialism, Marx went on to develop a materialist conception of history and explained it dialectically. Going a step further, he insisted that "the philosophers have only *interpreted* the world, in various ways; the point, however, is to *change* it." Thus, dialectical and historical materialism, committed to a scientific analysis of society *and* its transformation, became the hallmark of the Marxist approach that has set the broader parameters of discussion and debate in social theory over the past century.

The ongoing controversies in sociology and the other social sciences on the nature of contemporary society, economy, and polity are an extension of these earlier debates and have yielded a variety of diverse theoretical approaches, including Parsonian, Millsian, Althusserian, neo-Weberian, neo-Marxist, and "postmodernist" formulations. Herein lies the importance of classical and contemporary social theory, which has contributed in different ways to the totality of the knowledge we have come to obtain about society—a knowledge that is a direct product of the constant subjection of theory to the test of social reality.

The constant interaction of this continuously expanding theoretical knowledge with the changing conditions of social reality (i.e., between theory and practice) in the end informs our conception of different aspects of life in society—a process that highlights the importance of social theory as a tool for analysis to sort out the complex phenomena that define the nature and scope of human relations in society. For this reason, sociologists place great value on the pivotal role of social theory in the study of society.

BIBLIOGRAPHY

Althusser, Louis. 1971. "Ideology and Ideological State Apparatuses." In L. Althusser, *Lenin and Philosophy and Other Essays*. London: New Left Books.

———. 1976. *Essays in Self-Criticism*. London: New Left Books.

Althusser, Louis, and Etienne Balibar. 1968. *Reading Capital*. London: New Left Books.

Aptheker, Herbert. 1960. *The World of C. Wright Mills*. New York: Marzani and Munsell.

———. 1973. *Annotated Bibliography of the Published Writings of W.E.B. Du Bois*. Millwood, N.Y.: Kraus–Thomson.

———. 1990. "W.E.B. Du Bois: Struggle Not Despair." *Clinical Sociology Review* 8.

Bellah, Robert N. 1959. "Durkheim and History." *American Sociological Review* 24, no. 4 (August).

Berberoglu, Berch. 1990. *Political Sociology*. Dix Hills, N.Y.: General Hall.

———. 1991. *Critical Perspectives in Sociology*. Dubuque, Iowa: Kendall/Hunt.

———. 1992. *The Legacy of Empire: Economic Decline and Class Polarization in the United States*. New York: Praeger.

———. 1992. *The Political Economy of Development*. Albany, N.Y.: SUNY Press.

———. 1993. *The Labor Process and Control of Labor: The Changing Nature of Work Relations in the Late 20th Century*. New York: Praeger.

Birnbaum, Norman. 1971. *Toward a Critical Sociology*. New York: Oxford University Press.

Blackwell, James E., and Morris Janowitz, eds. 1974. *Black Sociologists: Historical and Contemporary Perspectives*. Chicago: University of Chicago Press.

Block, Fred. 1977. "The Ruling Class Does Not Rule: Notes on the Marxist Theory of the State." *Socialist Review*, no. 33 (May–June).

———. 1977. "Marxist Theories of the State in World System Analysis." Paper presented at the First Annual Political Economy of the World System Conference, American University, Washington, D.C.

———. 1978. "Class Consciousness and Capitalist Rationalization: A Reply to Critics." *Socialist Review*, nos. 40–41 (July–October).

———. 1987. *Revising State Theory*. Philadelphia: Temple University Press.

Bottomore, T.B. 1966. *Elites and Society*. Baltimore: Penguin.

Bottomore, Tom, and Robert J. Brym, eds. 1989. *The Capitalist Class: An International Study*. New York: New York University Press.

Callinicos, Alex. 1989. *Against Postmodernism: A Marxist Critique*. New York: St. Martin's Press.

Calvert, Peter. 1982. *The Concept of Class*. New York: St. Martin's Press.

145

Carnoy, Martin. 1984. *The State and Political Theory*. Princeton: Princeton University Press.

Clarke, S. 1977. "Marxism, Sociology and Poulantzas's Theory of the State." *Capital and Class* 2.

Comte, Auguste. 1893. *The Positive Philosophy*. London: Kegan Paul.

Cooper, John Milton, Jr. 1986. "Foreword." Manning Marable, *W.E.B. Du Bois: Black Radical Democrat*. Boston: Twayne.

Crompton, Rosemary, and Jon Gubbay. 1978. *Economy and Class Structure*. New York: St. Martin's Press.

Dahrendorf, Ralph. 1959. *Class and Class Conflict in Industrial Society*. Stanford: Stanford University Press.

Davis, Kingsley, and Wilbert E. Moore, 1945. "Some Principles of Stratification." *American Sociological Review* 10, no. 2 (April).

Dazhina, I.M., et al., eds. 1984. *Alexandra Kollontai: Selected Articles and Speeches*. New York: International Publishers.

Deegan, Mary Jo, ed. 1991. *Women in Sociology*. Westport, Conn.: Greenwood Press.

Domhoff, G. William. 1967. *Who Rules America?* Englewood Cliffs, N.J.: Prentice Hall.

———. 1971. *The Higher Circles: The Governing Class in America*. New York: Vintage.

———. 1978. *The Powers That Be: Processes of Ruling Class Domination in America*. New York: Vintage.

———. 1983. *Who Rules America Now? A View for the '80s*. New York: Simon & Schuster.

———. 1990. *The Power Elite and the State*. New York: Aldine de Gruyter.

Domhoff, G. William, and Hoyt B. Ballard, eds. 1968. *C.Wright Mills and the Power Elite*. Boston: Beacon Press.

Draper, Hal. 1977. *Karl Marx's Theory of Revolution: State and Bureaucracy*. Pts. 1 and 2. New York: Monthly Review Press.

Du Bois, W.E.B. 1953. "Negroes and the Crisis of Capitalism in the United States." *Monthly Review* 4 (April).

———. 1970. "The Social Effects of Emancipation" and "The Class Struggle." in *W.E.B. Du Bois: A Reader*, ed. Meyer Weinberg. New York: Harper & Row.

———. 1975. "The White Masters of the World." In *The Writings of W.E.B. Du Bois*, ed. Virginia Hamilton. New York: Crowell.

Durkheim, Emile. 1951. *Suicide: A Study in Sociology*. New York: Free Press.

———. 1957. *The Elementary Forms of Religious Life*. London: Allen & Unwin.

———. 1958. *Professional Ethics and Civic Morals*. Glencoe, Ill.: Free Press.

———. 1961. *Moral Education*. New York: Free Press of Glencoe.

———. 1964. *The Division of Labor in Society*. New York: Free Press.

Engels, Frederick. 1972. *The Origin of the Family, Private Property and the State*. In Karl Marx and Frederick Engels, *Selected Works*. New York: International Publishers.

———. 1972. *Ludwig Feuerbach and the End of Classical German Philosophy*. In Karl Marx and Frederick Engels, *Selected Works*. New York: International Publishers.

————. 1973. *The Peasant War in Germany*. New York: International Publishers.

————. 1976. *Anti-Duhring*. New York: International Publishers.

Esping-Andersen, Gosta, Roger Friedland, and Erik Olin Wright. 1976. "Modes of Class Struggle and the Capitalist State." *Kapitalistate*, nos. 4–5 (Summer).

Frazier, E. Franklin. 1939. *The Negro Family in the United States*. Chicago: University of Chicago Press.

————. 1949. *The Negro in the United States*. New York: Macmillan.

————. 1957. *Race and Culture Contacts in the Modern World*. New York: Knopf.

————. 1957. *Black Bourgeoisie*. Glencoe, Ill.: The Free Press.

Freud, Sigmund. 1949. *An Outline of Psychoanalysis*. New York: Norton.

————. 1950. *The Question of Lay Analysis*. New York: Norton.

————. 1961. *The Future of an Illusion*. Garden City, N.Y.: Doubleday Anchor.

————. 1962. *Civilization and Its Discontents*. New York: Norton.

Fromm, Erich. 1962. *Beyond the Chains of Illusion*. New York: Simon and Schuster.

————. 1970. *The Crisis of Psychoanalysis*. New York: Holt Rinehart, Winston.

Giddens, Anthony. 1971. *Capitalism and Modern Social Theory*. New York: Cambridge University Press.

Gold, David, Clarence Y.H. Lo, and Erik Olin Wright. 1975. "Some Recent Developments in Marxist Theories of the Capitalist State." Pts. 1 and 2. *Monthly Review* 27, nos. 5 and 6 (October and November).

Gouldner, Alvin W. 1970. *The Coming Crisis of Western Sociology*. New York: Avon Books.

Gramsci, Antonio. 1971. *Prison Notebooks*. New York: International Publishers.

————. 1978. *Selections from Political Writings 1921–26*. London: Lawrence & Wishart.

Habermas, Jurgen. 1975. *Legitimation Crisis*. Boston: Beacon Press.

Harvey, David. 1982. *The Limits to Capital*. Cambridge, Mass.: Basil Blackwell.

————. 1989. *The Condition of Postmodernity*. Cambridge, Mass.: Basil Blackwell.

Hegel, G.W.F. 1956. *The Philosophy of History*. New York: Dover.

————. 1969. *Science of Logic*. London: Allen and Unwin.

Holloway, John, and Sol Picciotto. 1977. "Capital, Crisis and the State." *Capital and Class*, no. 2.

————. 1979. "Introduction: Towards a Marxist Theory of the State." In *State and Capital*, ed. John Holloway and Sol Picciotto. London: Edward Arnold.

Holt, Alix, ed. 1978. *Selected Writings of Alexandra Kollontai*. Westport, Conn.: Lawrence Hill.

Hopkins, Terence K., and Immanuel Wallerstein. 1982. *World-Systems Analysis*. Beverly Hills, Calif.: Sage Publications.

Horne, Gerald. 1986. *Black & Red: W.E.B. Du Bois and the Afro-American Response to the Cold War, 1944–1963*. Albany, N.Y.: SUNY Press.

Horowitz, Irving Louis, ed. 1963. *Power, Politics and People*. New York: Oxford University Press.

Hume, David. 1949. *A Treatise of Human Nature*. Oxford: Claredon Press.

Jay, Martin. 1973. *The Dialectical Imagination*. Boston: Little, Brown.

Jessop, Bob. 1982. *The Capitalist State*. New York: New York University Press.

Kant, Immanuel. 1929. *Critique of Pure Reason*. New York: St. Martin's Press.

Kollontai, Alexandra. 1978. "The Social Basis of the Woman Question." In *Selected Writings of Alexandra Kollontai*, Alix Holt. Westport, Conn.: Lawrence Hill.

———. 1978. "Sexual Relations and the Class Struggle." In *Selected Writings of Alexandra Kollontai*, ed. Alix Holt. Westport, Conn.: Lawrence Hill.

Kuhn, Thomas S. 1970. *The Structure of Scientific Revolutions.* 2nd ed. Chicago: University of Chicago Press.

Lenin, V.I. 1947. *Works.* Vol. 31. Moscow: Foreign Languages Publishing House.

———. 1971. *Selected Works.* New York: International Publishers.

———. 1971. *What Is To Be Done?* In V.I. Lenin, *Selected Works.* New York: International Publishers.

———. 1971. *Imperialism, The Highest Stage of Capitalism.* In V.I. Lenin, *Selected Works.* New York: International Publishers.

———. 1971. *The State and Revolution.* In V.I. Lenin, *Selected Works.* New York: International Publishers.

———. 1974. *The State.* In Karl Marx, Frederick Engels, and V.I. Lenin, *On Historical Materialism.* New York: International Publishers.

———. 1975. *Selected Works in Three Volumes.* Vol. 2. Moscow: Progress Publishers.

McNall, Scott G., ed. 1979. *Theoretical Perspectives in Sociology.* New York: St. Martin's Press.

Manuel, Frank E. 1956. *The New World of Henri Saint-Simon.* Cambridge, Mass.: Harvard University Press.

Marable, Manning. 1986. *W.E.B. Du Bois: Black Radical Democrat.* Boston: Twayne.

Marcuse, Herbert. 1964. *One Dimensional Man.* Boston: Beacon Press.

———. 1968. *Eros and Civilization.* New York: Vintage Books.

Marger, Martin N. 1987. *Elites and Masses: An Introduction to Political Sociology.* 2nd ed. Belmont, Calif.: Wadsworth.

Markham, F.M.H. 1952. *Henri Comte de Saint-Simon.* Oxford, England: Basil Blackwell.

Marx, Karl. 1963. *The Poverty of Philosophy.* New York: International Publishers.

———. 1965. *Pre-Capitalist Economic Formations.* New York: International Publishers.

———. 1967. *Capital.* 3 vols. New York: International Publishers.

———. 1972. "Preface to *A Contribution to the Critique of Political Economy.*" In Karl Marx and Frederick Engels, *Selected Works.* New York: International Publishers.

Marx, K., and F. Engels. 1947. *The German Ideology.* New York: International Publishers.

———. 1972. "Manifesto of the Communist Party." In Karl Marx and Frederick Engels, *Selected Works.* New York: International Publishers.

Mead, George Herbert. 1934. *Mind, Self, and Society.* Chicago: University of Chicago Press.

Merton, Robert K. 1968. *Social Theory and Social Structure.* New York: Free Press.

Michels, Robert. 1968. *Political Parties.* New York: Free Press.

Miliband, Ralph. 1969. *The State in Capitalist Society.* New York: Basic Books.

——. 1970. "The Capitalist State—Reply to Nicos Poulantzas." *New Left Review*, no. 59.

——. 1973. "Poulantzas and the Capitalist State." *NewLeft Review*, no. 82.

——. 1975. "Political Forms and Historical Materialism." In *Socialist Register*, ed. R. Miliband and J. Saville. London: Merlin Press.

——. 1977. *Marxism and Politics*. London: Oxford University Press.

——. 1982. *Capitalist Democracy in Britain*. London: Oxford University Press.

Mills, C. Wright. 1951. *White Collar: The American Middle Classes*. New York: Oxford University Press.

——. 1956. *The Power Elite*. New York: Oxford University Press.

——. 1959. *The Sociological Imagination*. New York: Oxford University Press.

Mollenkopf, John. 1975. "Theories of the State and Power Structure Research." *Insurgent Sociologist* 5, no. 3.

Mosca, Gaetano. 1939. *The Ruling Class*. New York: McGraw-Hill.

Oberndorf, C.P. 1953. *A History of Psychoanalysis in America*. New York: Grune.

Palmer, Bryan D. 1990. *Descent into Discourse*. Philadelphia: Temple University Press.

Parenti, Michael. 1970. "Power and Pluralism: The View from the Bottom." *Journal of Politics* 32 (August).

——. 1988. *Democracy for the Few*. 5th ed. New York: St. Martin's Press.

Pareto, Vilfredo. 1935. *The Mind and Society*. 4 vols. New York: Harcourt, Brace.

Parsons, Talcott. 1951. *The Social System*. New York: Free Press.

——. 1960. *Structure and Process in Modern Societies*. New York: Free Press.

——. 1966. *Societies: An Evolutionary Approach*. Englewood Cliffs, N.J.: Prentice Hall.

——. 1967. "On the Concept of Political Power." In T. Parsons, *Sociological Theory and Modern Society*. New York: Free Press.

Picciotto, Sol. 1979. "The Theory of the State, Class Struggle, and the Rule of Law." In *Capitalism and the Rule of Law*, ed. Ben Fine et al. London: Hutchinson.

Platt, Anthony M. 1991. *E. Franklin Frazier Reconsidered*. New Brunswick, N.J.: Rutgers University Press.

Polanyi, Karl. 1957. *The Great Transformation*. Boston: Beacon.

Poulantzas, Nicos. 1969. "The Problem of the Capitalist State." *New Left Review*, no. 58.

——. 1973. *Political Power and Social Classes*. London: Verso.

——. 1974. *Fascism and Dictatorship*. London: New Left Books.

——. 1975. *Classes in Contemporary Capitalism*. London: New Left Books.

——. 1976. *The Crisis of the Dictatorships*. London: New Left Books.

——. 1976. "The Capitalist State: A Reply to Miliband and Laclau." *New Left Review*, no. 95.

——. 1978. *State, Power, Socialism*. London: Verso.

——. 1979. "The Political Crisis and the Crisis of the State." In *Critical Sociology: European Perspectives*, ed. J.W. Freiberg. New York: Irvington.

Reich, Wilhelm. 1949. *Character Analysis*. New York: Orgone Institute Press.

——. 1970. *The Mass Psychology of Fascism*. New York: Farrar, Strauss and Giroux.

——. 1972. *Sex Pol; Essays, 1929–1934*. New York: Random House.

Reynolds, Larry T., and Janice M. Reynolds, eds. 1970. *The Sociology of Sociology.* New York: McKay.

Ross, Robert J.S., and Kent C. Trachte. 1990. *Global Capitalism: The New Leviathan.* Albany, N.Y.: SUNY Press.

Rousseau, Jean Jacques. 1950. *The Social Contract.* New York: Dutton.

Rowbotham, Sheila. 1972. *Women, Resistance, and Revolution.* New York: Penguin.

Saint-Simon, Henri de. 1964. *Social Organization, the Science of Man and Other Writings.* New York: Harper and Row.

Skocpol, Theda. 1979. *States and Revolutions: A Comparative Analysis of France, Russia and China.* Cambridge, England: Cambridge University Press.

———. 1981. "Political Response to Capitalist Crisis: Neo-Marxist Theories of the State and the Case of the New Deal." *Politics and Society* 10, no. 2.

Smith, Tony. 1990. *The Logic of Marx's Capital.* Albany, N.Y.: SUNY Press.

So, Alvin Y. 1990. *Social Change and Development.* Newbury Park, Calif.: Sage Publications.

Szymanski, Albert. 1976. "The Revolutionary Uses of Freudian Theory." *Social Praxis* 5, nos. 1–2.

———. 1978. *The Capitalist State and the Politics of Class.* Cambridge, Mass.: Winthrop.

———. 1981. *The Logic of Imperialism.* New York: Praeger.

———. 1983. *Class Structure: A Critical Perspective.* New York: Praeger.

Therborn, Goran. 1976. *Science, Class and Society.* London: New Left Books.

———. 1977. "The Rule of Capital and the Rise of Democracy." *New Left Review,* no. 103.

———. 1978. *What Does the Ruling Class Do When It Rules?* London: New Left Books.

———. 1980. *The Ideology of Power and the Power of Ideology.* London: New Left Books.

———. 1986. "Neo-Marxist, Pluralist, Corporatist, Statist Theories and the Welfare State." In *The State in Global Perspective,* ed. A. Kazancigil. Aldershot, England: Gower and UNESCO.

Trimberger, Ellen K. 1978. *Revolution from Above: Military Bureaucrats and Development in Japan, Turkey, and Peru.* New Brunswick, N.J.: Transaction Books.

Tumin, Melvin. 1953. "Some Principles of Stratification: A Critical Analysis." *American Sociological Review* 18, no. 4 (August).

Turner, Jonathan H. 1978. *The Structure of Sociological Theory.* Homewood, Ill.: Dorsey Press.

Wallerstein, Immanuel. 1974. *The Modern World System.* New York: Academic Press.

———. 1974. "The Rise and Future Demise of the World Capitalist System." *Comparative Studies in Society and History* 16 (September).

———. 1979. *The Capitalist World-Economy.* Cambridge, England: Cambridge University Press.

Walton, John. 1990. *Sociology and Critical Inquiry.* 2nd ed. Belmont, Calif.: Wadsworth.

Weber, Max. 1948. *The Protestant Ethic and the Spirit of Capitalism.* New York: Scribners.

———. 1964. *The Theory of Social and Economic Organization.* Edited and with an introduction by Talcott Parsons. New York: Free Press.

———. 1967. *From Max Weber. Essays in Sociology.* Trans., ed., and with an intro. by H.H. Gerth and C. Wright Mills. New York: Oxford University Press.

———. 1968. *Economy and Society.* 3 vols. New York: Bedminster Press.

Weinberg, Meyer, ed. 1970. *W.E.B. Du Bois: A Reader.* New York: Harper & Row.

Wells, Harry K. 1963. *The Failure of Psychoanalysis.* New York: International Publishers.

Westby, David L. 1991. *The Growth of Sociological Theory.* Englewood Cliffs, N.J.: Prentice Hall.

Willie, Charles V., ed. 1989. *The Caste and Class Controversy on Race and Poverty.* Dix Hills, N.Y.: General Hall.

Wilson, William Julius. 1978. *The Declining Significance of Race.* Chicago: University of Chicago Press.

———. 1987. *The Truly Disadvantaged: The Inner City, the Underclass, and Public Policy.* Chicago: University of Chicago Press.

Wolff, Kurt H., ed. 1960. *Emile Durkheim, 1858–1917.* Columbus: Ohio State University Press.

Wright, Erik Olin. 1974–75. "To Control or To Smash Bureaucracy: Weber and Lenin on Politics, the State, and Bureaucracy." *Berkeley Journal of Sociology* 19.

———. 1978. *Class, Crisis and the State.* London: New Left Books.

———. 1985. *Classes.* London: Verso.

Zeitlin, Irving M. 1968. *Ideology and the Development of Sociological Theory.* Englewood Cliffs, N.J.: Prentice Hall.

———. 1973. *Rethinking Sociology: A Critique of Contemporary Theory.* Englewood Cliffs, N.J.: Prentice Hall.

———. 1981. *The Social Condition of Humanity.* New York: Oxford University Press.

ABOUT THE AUTHOR

Berch Berberoglu is professor of sociology at the University of Nevada, Reno, where he has been teaching for the past sixteen years.

Dr. Berberoglu has authored and edited twelve books and many articles in numerous scholarly journals. His recent books include *The Internationalization of Capital* (1987), *Political Sociology: A Comparative/Historical Approach* (1990), *Critical Perspectives in Sociology* (1991), *The Legacy of Empire: Economic Decline and Class Polarization in the United States* (1992), *The Political Economy of Development* (1992), and *The Labor Process and Control of Labor: The Changing Nature of Work Relations in the Late 20th Century* (1993).

He is currently doing research and writing on the world political economy titled *The European and Japanese Challenge: Global Rivalry and the Rise of the Old Powers in the Late 20th Century* and is preparing a new book on class structure titled *Class Analysis: Class Conflict and Social Transformation*, both of which are scheduled for publication in 1994.

Dr. Berberoglu received his Ph.D. from the University of Oregon in 1977 and his B.S. and M.A. from Central Michigan University in 1972 and 1974. He also did graduate work at the State University of New York at Binghamton in the early 1970s.

Index

153